Anonymous

Missionary Hymnal

For the Use of Junior and Juvenile Missionar Societies

Anonymous

Missionary Hymnal
For the Use of Junior and Juvenile Missionar Societies

ISBN/EAN: 9783337372149

Printed in Europe, USA, Canada, Australia, Japan

Cover: Foto ©Thomas Meinert / pixelio.de

More available books at **www.hansebooks.com**

THE

MISSIONARY HYMNAL.

FOR THE USE OF

JUNIOR AND JUVENILE

MISSIONARY SOCIETIES.

———————— ‹‹◦◊◦›› ————————

PUBLISHED BY THE
WOMAN'S BOARD OF MISSIONS OF THE INTERIOR,
CHICAGO.
1888.

PREFACE.

In offering this little volume of Hymns to our Juniors and Leaders of Mission Bands, the compilers would earnestly call the attention of those who use it, to one or two practical suggestions.

Our object has been to gather helpful, devotional and more positively Missionary Hymns set to appropriate and choice music.

Some of the tunes are old and well known, many are quite simple and can be readily sung, while others may not, at first, commend themselves, because they seem difficult, but these will grow in favor and interest as they become familiar. Such songs should never be attempted in open meeting without previous practice.

Indeed the song service of a meeting is worthy of the same preparation which is given to other parts of it, and when we learn that the singing cannot go of itself, our meetings will almost never fail in interest. We would suggest that those most proficient in music should come together and practice in advance. A nucleus thus formed of those able to render intelligently both words and music, will make it easy for others to follow.

We extend our hearty thanks to all the friends of the Woman's Board of Missions of the Interior, whose words of encouragement have cheered our work, and especially to those whose gifts of hymns and music have enabled us to publish the book without laying upon the Board any burden of expense.

That it may become a helpful instrument in the deepening and extension of missionary interest, and so hasten the coming of the kingdom of our Lord is the earnest hope of

The Committee.

MISSIONARY HYMNAL.

CONSECRATION.

F. R. HAVERGAL. REINECKE.

1. Take my life and let it be Con - se - cra - ted, Lord, to
2. Take my feet and let them be Swift and beau - ti - ful for
3. Take my lips and let them be Fill'd with mes - sa - ges from
4. Take my love, my Lord, I pour At Thy feet its treas - ure

Thee; Take my hands and let them move At the im - pulse of thy love.
Thee; Take my voice and let me sing, Always, on - ly, for my King.
Thee; Take my sil - ver and my gold, Not a mite would I with-hold.
store; Take my-self and I will be Ev - er, on - ly, all for Thee.

4

Henry Francis Lyte, 1834.

Sir. Arthur Sullivan.

1. O that the Lord's sal - va - tion Were out of Zi - on come,
2. Let fall Thy rod of ter - ror, Thy sav - ing grace im - part;

To heal His an - cient Na - tion, To lead His out - cast home.
Roll back the veil of er - ror, Re - lease the fet - tered heart.

How long the Ho - ly Cit - y Shall heath - en feet pro - fane?
Let Is - rael, home re - turn - ing, Her lost Mes - si - ah see;

Re - turn, O Lord, in pit - y; Re - build her walls a - gain.
Give oil of joy for mourning, And bind Thy church to Thee.

E. C. Brewer. C. Reinecke.

1. Lit - tle drops of wa - ter, Lit - tle grains of sand,
2. Thus the lit - tle min - utes, Hum - ble tho' they be,
3. Lit - tle deeds of kind - ness, Lit - tle words of love,
4. Lit - tle seeds of mer - cy, Sown by youth-ful hands,

Make the might-y o - cean, And the pleas-ant land.
Make the might-y a - ges, Of e - ter - ni - ty.
Make our earth an E - den, Like the heav'n a - bove.
Grow to bless the na - tions Far in heath-en lands.

Auon.   C. Reinecke.

1. Lit - tle giv - ers, come and bring   Tri- bute
2. Lit - tle giv - ers, do your part,   With a
3. Give to   all   the   dark - ened earth,   Ti - dings

to   your heav'n-ly King;   Lay it on   the   al - tar
glad and   will - ing heart; For the an - gel voic - es
of   a   heav'n-ly birth; Till the youth in   ev - 'ry

high, While your songs as - cend the sky, Lay it
say, Lit - tle giv - ers, give to - day, For the
land, Learn the Sav - ior's sweet com - mand, Till the

on the al - tar high, While your songs as - cend the sky.
an - gel voic - es say, Lit - tle giv - ers, give to - day.
youth in ev - 'ry land, Learn the Sav - ior's sweet command.

8

Rev. S. Baring Gould, 1865.

Arthur S. Sullivan.

1. On - ward, Chris-tian sol - diers, March-ing as to war,
2. Like a might-y ar - my Moves the church of God;
3. Crowns and thrones may per - ish, King - doms rise and wane,
4. On - ward, then, ye peo - ple, Join our hap - py throng,

With the cross of Je - sus Go - ing on be - fore;
Broth - ers, we are tread - ing Where the saints have trod;
But the church of Je - sus Con - stant will re - main;
Blend with ours your voic - es In the tri - umph song;

Christ, the Roy - al Mas - ter, Leads a - gainst the foe;
We are not di - vid - ed, All one bod - y we,
Gates of hell can nev - er 'Gainst that church pre - vail;
Glo - ry, laud and hon - or Un - to Christ, the King,

For - ward in - to bat - tle See His ban - ner go.
One in hope and doc - trine, One in char - i - ty.
We have Christ's own prom - ise, And that can - not fail.
This thro' count - less a - ges, Men and an - gels sing.

On - ward, Chris - tian sol - diers, March-ing as to war,

With the cross of Je - sus Go - ing on be - fore.

HEROLD.

Rev. Leonard Bacon, D. D., 1833.

Arranged.

1. Wake the song of ju - bi - lee, Let it ech - o o'er the sea;
2. Hark the des - ert lands re-joice, And the isl - ands join their voice;

Now is come the prom-ised hour; Je - sus reigns with glo - rious pow'r.
Joy! the whole cre - a - tion sings, "Je - sus is the King of kings."

All ye na-tions, join and sing, Praise your Sav-ior, praise your King;
Praise the name of God most high, Praise Him, all be - low the sky,

Let it sound from shore to shore, "Jesus reigns for ev - er more."
Praise Him all ye heav'n - ly host, Father, Son and Ho - ly Ghost.

11

CUTTING.

S. Wolcott, 1869. W. F. Sherwin, by per.

1. Christ for the world we sing; The world to Christ we bring,
2. Christ for the world we sing; The world to Christ we bring,
3. Christ for the world we sing; The world to Christ we bring,
4. Christ for the world we sing; The world to Christ we bring,

With loving zeal, The poor, and them that mourn, The faint and
With fervent pray'r; The way - ward and the lost, By rest - less
With one ac - cord; With us the work to share, With us re -
With joy - ful song; The new - born souls whose days, Reclaimed from

o - ver borne, Sin - sick and sor-row-worn, Whom Christ doth heal.
pas - sions tossed, Re-deemed at countless cost, From dark de - spair.
proach to dare, With us the cross to bear, For Christ our Lord.
er - ror's ways, In-spired with hope and praise, To Christ be - long.

MISSIONARY CHANT.

Isaac Watts, 1719.

Chas. Zeuner, 1832.

1. Je - sus shall reign where e'er the sun, Does
2. For Him shall end - less pray'r be made, And
3. Peo - ple and realms of ev - ry tongue, Dwell
4. Bles - sings a - bound where e'er He reigns; The
5. Let ev - 'ry crea - ture rise and bring Pe -

his suc - ces - sive jour - neys run; His king-dom
end - less prais - es crown His head, His name, like
on His love with sweet - est song; And in - fant
pris - 'ner leaps to loose his chains The wea - ry
cu - liar hon - ors to our King; An - gels de

stretch from shore to shore, Till moons shall wax and wane no more.
sweet per-fume, shall rise With ev - ry morn-ing sac - ri - fice.
voi - ces shall proclaim, Their ear - ly bless-ings on His name.
find e - ter - nal rest And all the sons of want are blest.
scend with songs a-gain, And earth re - peat the loud a - men.

Anon, 1829   Tune "MISSIONARY CHANT.

1 Soon may the last glad song arise
   Through all the millions of the skies,
   That song of triumph which records
   That all the earth is now the Lord's.

2 Let thrones and powers and kingdoms be
   Obedient, mighty God to thee ;
   And over land and sea and main,
   Wave Thou the sceptre of Thy reign.

3 O let the glorious anthem swell,
   Let host to host the triumph tell,
   That not one rebel heart remains
   But over all the Savior reigns.

MIRA.

Mrs. K. H. Johnson, by per.

Fred. L. Morey.

1. Hap - py are we, God's own lit - tle flock,
2. What shall we do, for the Mas - ter so dear?
3. Man - y He has who are not in the fold,
4. O - ver the moun - tains, o - ver the seas,
5 Joy - ful - ly then, let us spread the glad news,

Shel - ter'd so close in tho cleft of the rock;
O! there arc man - y in need of our cheer,
Out in the storm and the pit - i - less cold;
Lov - ing - ly, joy - ful - ly, speed we to these,
Nev - er this ser - vice for Je - sus re - fuse,

Far a - bove storm or dan - ger or shock,
Souls that know noth-ing, but dark - ness and fear,
These we will win by our pray'rs and our gold,
Seek-ing to save them by ten - der - est pleas,
Nev - er a mo - ment to work for him lose,

Hap - py are we with Je - sus.
Souls in the dark with-out Je - sus.
Win them to love our Je - sus.
Save by the blood of Je - sus.
Joy - ful - ly work for Je - sus.

BITTER SWEET.

Anon.

REV. W. A. BARTLETT.

1. Pit - y the children a - cross the sea, Who nev - er the
2. Pit - y the children a - cross the sea. The Mas - ter pro-

name of Christ have heard. Who i - dols wor - ship on
- claims in a voice of love, "Suf - fer the chil - dren to

bend - ed knee, Which see not and hear not a sin - gle word.
come to me, Of such is the king - dom of God a - bove."

1. Gra - cious Spir - it, dwell with me,— I, my - self, would gra - cious be; And with words that help and heal, Would Thy life in mine re - veal; And with ac - tions bold and meek, Would for Christ my Sav - ior speak.

2. Truth - ful Spir - it, dwell with me,— I, my - self, would truth - ful be; And with wis - dom kind and clear, Let Thy life in mine ap - pear; And with ac - tion broth - er - ly, Speak my Lord's sin - cer - i - ty.

3. Ten - der Spir - it, dwell with me,— I, my - self, would ten - der be; Shut my heart up like a flow'r, At temp - ta - tion's dark-some hour: O - pen it when shines the sun, And His love by fra - grance own.

4. Ho - ly Spir - it, dwell with me,— I, my - self, would ho - ly be; Sep - a - rate from sin I would Choose and cher - ish all things good; And what-ev - er I can be, Give to Him who gave me Thee.

Anon.   MISSION BAND RALLYING SONG.

1. We're a   band   of   mis - sion   work - ers   in   the
2. We   hear   the   tramp   of   mill - ions   like   the
3. Yes,   all   the   world   for   Je - - - sus,   for

ser - vice of   our King; Our   hearts, our hands, our voi - ces, our
ris - ing tem-pest's roar, Like the sound of man - y wa - ters as they
all   the world He died, He   loves the heath - en chil-dren and will

pen - nies, too,   we bring; And we'll   make   the   earth   be-
break up - on   the shore; They·   come   from   dis - tant
bring them to   His side, Then He'll   lay   His   hands   up-

neath us and the heav'n a - bove us ring, As we go march-ing on.
na-tions and are com-ing more and more, As we go march-ing on.
on them, and in columns deep. and wide We'll all go march-ing on.

CHORUS.

Glo - ry, glo - ry, hal - le - lu - jah! Glo - ry, glo - ry, hal - le - lu - jah!

Glo - ry, glo - ry, hal - le - lu - jah, As we go march-ing on.

BUILDER'S HYMN.

Dedicated to the "Engineer of the Bridge."

ELLA G. IVES.

1 In the freshness of the morning, in the glory of our youth,
With our hearts alert for service and our souls on fire for truth,
We are coming, we are coming, with this song in every mouth,
God's kingdom marches on.

CHO. Glory, glory, hallelujah, glory, glory, hallelujah,
Glory, glory, hallelujah, God's kingdom marches on.

2 A highway we are building for the ransomed of the Lord,
With the cross for its foundation and its arches of the Word:
It shall bridge the widest chasm with the promises of God,
Whose kingdom marches on. CHO.

3 Across the mighty continents and o'er the pathless sea,
We are stretching massive arches that shall last eternally;
And along the shining pathway press the footsteps of the free,
Whose souls are marching on. CHO.

4 From Orient and Occident these children of a King,
To claim a royal heritage, their souls from bondage bring:
And as they seek their Father's House, their happy voices ring,
Our souls are marching on. CHO.

20

F. W. HARRIS.

J. STAINER, 1872.

1. Je - sus, high in glo - ry, Lend a list-'ning ear,
2. Save us, Lord, from sin - ning, Watch us, day by day;

When we bow be - fore Thee, Chil-dren's prais - es hear;
Help us now to love Thee, Take our sins a - way;

Tho' Thou art so ho - ly Heav'n's Al-might - y King,
Then when Je - sus calls us To our heav'n-ly home,

Thou wilt stoop to list - en; When Thy praise we sing.
We would glad - ly an - swer, Sav - ior, Lord, we come.

JEWELS.

Rev. W. O. Cushing.   Geo. F. Root.

1. When he com - eth, When he com - eth To make up His
2. He will gath - er, He will gath - er, The gems for His
3. Lit - tle chil - dren, Lit - tle chil - dren, Who love their Re -

jew - els, All His jew - els, precious jew - els, His lov'd and His own.
king - dom: All the pure ones, all the bright ones, His lov'd and His own.
deem - er, Are the jew - els, precious jew - els, His lov'd and His own.

Chorus.

Like the stars of the morn - ing, His bright crown a -

dorn-ing, They shall shine in their beau -ty, Bright gems for His crown.

H. Bonar, 1857.

Louis Spohr.
Arr. by Barnby, 1867.

1. I heard the voice of Je - sus say, "Come
2. I heard the voice of Je - sus say, "Be -
3. I heard the voice of Je - sus say, "I

un - to me and rest; Lay down, thou wea - ry
-hold, I free - ly give. The liv - ing wa - ter!
am this dark world's light; Look un - to me; thy

one, lay down Thy head up - on my breast."
thirst - y one, Stoop down, and drink and live."
morn shall rise And all thy days be bright."

I came to Je - sus, as I was, Wea -
I came to Je - sus and I drank Of
I look'd to Je - sus and I found In

ry, and worn, and sad, I found in Him a
that life - giv - ing stream, My thirst was quenched, my
Him my Star, my Sun; And in that life of

rest - ing place, And He hath made me glad.
soul re - vived, And now I live in Him.
light I'll walk, Till all my jour - ney's done.

24

Mrs. Jemima Luke, 1841.

John Henry Cornell, 1871,

1. I think when I read that sweet sto - ry of old,
2. I wish that His hands had been placed on my head,
3. Yet still to His foot - stool in prayer I may go,
4. In that beau - ti - ful place He has gone to pre - pare,
5. But thou - sands and thou - sands, who wan - der and fall,
6. I long for the bless - ed and glo - ri - ous time

When Je - sus was here a - mong men,
That His arms had been thrown a - round me,
And ask for a share in His love;
For all who are washed and for - giv'n;
Nev - er heard of that heav - en - ly home;
The fair - est and bright - est and best,

By per. of J. B. Young & Co.

How He called lit - tle chil - dren as lambs to His fold,
And that I might have seen His kind look when He said,
And if I but earn - est - ly seek Him be - low,
And man - y dear chil - dren shall be with Him there,
I wish they could know there is room for them all,
When the dear lit - tle chil - dren of ev - er - y clime

I should like to have been with Him then,
"Let the lit - tle ones come un - to me."
I shall see Him and hear Him a - bove.
For "of such is the king - dom of heav'n."
And that Je - sus has bid them to come.
Shall crowd to His arms and be blessed.

ANGEL VOICES

Rev. Francis Pott, 1861.

Arthur Seymour Sullivan,

1. An - gel voic - es, ev - er sing - ing Round Thy throne of
2. Thou Who art be - yond the far - thest Mor - tal eye can
3. Yea, we know Thy love re - joic - es O'er each work of
4. Here, great God, to - day we of - fer Of Thine own to
5. Hon - or, glo - ry, might and mer - it, Thine shall ev - er

light, An - gel harps for - ev - er ring - ing,
scan, Can it be that Thou re - gard - est
Thine; Thou did'st ears and hands and voic - es
Thee; And for Thine ac - cept - ance prof - fer,
be, Fa - ther, Son and Ho - ly Spir - it,

Rest not day nor night, Thous-ands on - ly
Songs of sin - ful man? Can we feel that
For Thy praise com - bine; Crafts-man's art and
All un - worth - i - ly; Hearts and minds, and
Bless - ed Trin - i - ty! Of the best that

live to bless Thee, And con - fess Thee, Lord of might.
Thou art near us And wilt hear us? Yea, we can.
mu-sic's meas - ure For Thy pleas-ure, Did'st de - sign.
hands and voic - es, In our choic - est Mel - o - dy.
Thou hast giv - en Earth and heav - en Ren - der Thee. A-men

HERRICK.

Mrs. Martha Tyler Gale.

Rev. C. S. Richards.

1. More pow'r to serve Thee, Lord, And spread Thy word;
2. Guide us in word and deed, Warm love we need,
3. A - lone we would not come To Heav'n our home,

Per - sua - sive pow'r to win Wan-d'rers from sin.
Large hearts em - brac - ing all To give Thy call.
But man - y tro - phies bring Our Sav - ior King.

This grace we now im-plore, Wis - dom to serve Thee more,
Give pow'r to help the weak, Like Thee most high, most meek;
What joy be - fore Thy throne, If Thou wilt say, "We'll done,"

Wis - dom to serve Thee more, Whom we a - dore.
Like Thee most high, most meek, The low - est seek.
If Thou wilt say "Well done, My faith - ful one."

By permission.

JESUS LOVES THE LITTLE CHILDREN

Anon.

Reinecke.

1. Je - sus loves the lit - tle chil - dren
2. There are man - y lit - tle chil - dren
3. I would tell these lit - tle chil - dren
4. Lis - ten, now, while we re - peat it,

For He said one day, "Let the chil - dren
Who have nev - er heard Of His love and
If they all could hear, How He spoke to
Hark! 'tis ver - y sweet, I should think 'twould

come to me, Keep them, not a - way."
ten - der - ness, Of His ho - ly word.
His dis - ci - ples With the chil - dren near.
make the chil-dren, Hast-en Him to meet.*

*Recite. "Suffer little children to come unto me, and forbid them not, for of such is the kingdom of heaven."

Mrs. Emily Huntington Miller.   James McGranahan.

1. Je - sus bids us shine With a clear, pure light,
2. Je - sus bids us shine First of all for Him,
3. Je - sus bids us shine Then for all a - round;

Like a lit - tle can - dle Burn - ing in the night;
Well He sees and knows it If our light is dim;
Man - y kinds of dark - ness In the world are found,

In the world is dark - ness, So we must shine,
He looks down from heav - en To see us shine,
Sin, and want and sor - row, So we must shine,

You in your lit - tle cor - ner, And I in mine.

Used by permission of The John Church Co, owners of the Copyright.

EVENING PRAYER.

MARY J. WILLCOX.

RANDEGGER.

1. Once a - gain, dear Lord, we pray, For the
2. Lit - tle lips that Thou hast made, 'Neath the
3. Lit - tle hands whose won - drous skill, Thou hast
4. Teach them, oh Thou heav - 'nly King, All their

chil-dren far a - way, Who have nev - er ev - en
far off tem - ple's shade, Give to gods of wood and
giv'n to do Thy will, Of - f'rings bring and serve with
gifts and praise to bring, To Thy Son, who died to

heard Je - sus' name, our sweet - est word.
stone, Praise that should be all Thine own.
fear, Gods that can - not see or hear.
prove, Thy for - giv - ing, sav - ing love.

Copyright, 1897.

GIVE THANKS.

Anon.

FRED. L. MOREY.

1. Give thanks, all Chris-tian peo - ple, The Lord has heard your
2. Good news to hea-then na - tions, On wings of faith is
3. He rends the gates of dark - ness, He pours the light with -

pray'r; Has o - pen'd wide the door - ways, That
borne, Sal - va - tion to the lost one, And
in, He rears the cross of Je - sus, Re -

CHORUS.

joice, re - joice and praise your King, His prais - es sweet - ly sing.

WE ARE HAPPY CHILDREN

ANON.

1. We are chil - dren, hap - py chil - dren, Sing - ing.
2. When a sin - ful world a - round us Tempts our
3. If we try to fol - low Je - sus, Try to

sing - ing, as we go, 'Tis our Fa - ther's
lit - tle feet to stray, By His Spir - it,
serve Him here be - low, Where He lives and

hand that leads us, Leads us, through this world be - low.
He will keep us In the straight and nar - row way.
reigns for - ev - er, Sing - ing, sing - ing we shall go,

From S. S. Hymnal, by per.

Anon.

German.

1. I can-not do great things for Him, Who did so much for me,
2. There are small things in dai-ly life, In which I may o-bey,
3. There are small cross-es I may take, Small bur-dens I may bear,
4. So I ask Thee to give me grace, My lit-tle place to fill,

But I should like to show my love, Dear Je-sus, un-to Thee;
And thus may show my love to Thee, And al-ways, ev-'ry day;
Small acts of faith and deeds of love, Some sor-rows I may share;
That I may ev-er walk with Thee, And ev-er do Thy will;

Faith-ful in ver-y lit-tle things, O Sav-ior, may I be,
There are some lit-tle lov-ing words, Which I for Thee may say,
And lit-tle bits of work for Thee, I may do ev-'ry where,
That in each du-ty, great or small, I may be faith-ful still,

Faith - ful in ver - y lit - tle things, O Sav - ior, may I be.
There are some lit - tle, lov - ing words, Which I for Thee may say.
And lit - tle bits of work for Thee, I may do ev - 'ry where.
That in each du - ty, great or small, I may be faith-ful still.

TUNE, "I Cannot do Great things for Him."

Anon.

1 What can I give to Jesus
   Who gave His life for me?
How can I show my love to Him
   Who died on Calvary?
I'll give my heart to Jesus,
   In childhood's tender Spring,
I know that He will not despise
   The offering that I bring.

2 I'll give my soul to Jesus
   And calmly, gladly rest,
Its youthful hopes and fond desires
   Upon His loving breast.
I'll give my mind to Jesus
   And seek in thoughtful hours
His spirit's grace to consecrate
   Its early opening powers.

3 I'll give my strength to Jesus
   Of foot, of head, of will;
Run where He sends and ever strive
   His pleasure to fulfil.
I'll give my time to Jesus;
   Oh that each hour might be
Filled up with holy work for Him,
   Who spent His life for me.

MENDEBRAS.

ESTHER THORNE, by per.

German.

1. Sav' - ior of lit - tle chil - dren, We
2. Praise for the love that sought us And
3. Praise for the lit - tle chil - dren, Borne
4. Lord, let us all, Thy chil - dren, Join

hail Thee, as our King! With joy - ful hearts and
led us home, to Thee: Praise, for the blood that
in Thine arms of love, Shin - ing like spot - less
their "new song" to - day! Teach us to do Thy

voic - es, Teach us Thy praise to sing.
bought us, Lambs of Thy flock to be;
lil - ies, Be - fore the throne a - - bove,
bid - ding, Teach us to praise and pray,

Copyright, 1887.

We bless Thee for cre - a - tion, For
Praise for the path to heav - en, Shin -
Ran - somed from ev' - ry na - tion, Joy -
Not with our voic - es on - ly, Though

life with bless - ings sweet, In grate - ful ad - or -
ing, to per - fect day; Praise for Thy Spir - it
ful the song they sing, "We bless Thee for sal -
as of an - gels sweet, But with our lives to

a - tion We bow be - fore Thy feet.
giv - en, To guide us all the way.
va - tion, We hail Thee, as our King."
bless Thee, We lay them at Thy feet.

STELLA.

Mrs. S. B. PRATT. by per.

German.

1. Once was heard the song of chil - dren, By the
2. Palms of vic - t'ry strewn a - round Him, Gar - ments
3. God o'er all in heav - en reign - ing, We this
4. Oh, though humble is our of - f'ring, Lord, ac -

Sav - ior when on earth; Joy - ful in the sa - cred
spread be - neath His feet, Pro - phet of the Lord, they
day Thy glo - ry sing; Not with palms Thy path - way
cept our grate - ful lays, These from chil - dren once pro -

tem - ple, Shouts of youth - ful praise had birth;
crown'd Him, In fair Sa - lem's crowd - ed street,
strew - ing, We would loft - ier trib - ute bring,
ceed - ing, Thou did'st deem most per - fect praise,

And Ho - san - nas, and Ho - san - nas, Loud to
While Ho - san - nas, while Ho - san - nas, From the
Glad Ho - san - nas, Glad Ho - san - nas, To our
Now Ho - san - nas, Now Ho - san - nas, Sav - ior,
Da - vid's Son broke forth, And Ho - san - nas, and Ho -
lips of chil - dren greet, While Ho - san - nas, while Ho -
Proph - et, Priest and King, Glad Ho - san - nas, glad Ho -
Lord, to Thee, we raise, Now Ho - san - nas, now Ho -
- san - nas, Loud, to Da - vid's son broke forth.
- san - nas, From the lips of chil - dren greet.
- san - nas, To our Proph - et, Priest and King.
- san - nas, Sav - ior, Lord, to Thee we raise.

LOCHBY.

Anon.

REV. W. A. BARTLETT, 1887.

1. We are a little glean-ing band, We cannot bind the sheaves, But we can fol-low Him Who reaps.And gath-er what He leaves, We are not strong,but Je-sus loves The weak-est of the fold, And

2. We are not rich, but we can give, As we are pass-ing on A cup of wa-ter in His name To some poor faint-ing one, We are not wise, but Christ, our Lord, Re-vealed to babes His will And

3. We know that with our gath-ered grain Bri-ars and leaves are seen, Yet, since we tried, He smiles the same, And takes our of-fer-ing, Dear chil-dren, still Ho-san-na sing, As Christ doth conquering come. Cast-

RALLYING SONG!

(Written expressly for the May Rally).

BY MRS. M. J. WILLCOX.

In faith and hope we gather here
  With courage strong and true,
And willing hearts that waiting seek
  Some work of love to do.
One Name our whole allegiance claims,
  The Name of Christ our Lord;
Beneath His Cross we rally now,
  To send His truth abroad.

Where India waves her feathery palms,
  Beneath the Crescent's might,
See woman, bowed in sorrow, wait
  The news of Life and Light.
The Love that gives us peace and rest,
  Would fold with circling arm
All these who suffer and have sinned,
  And keep them safe from harm.

Dear prisoned ones, we bring to-day
  The story ever new;
Our watchword—"Jesus died for all;"
  Our song—"He died for you."
One Name our whole allegiance claims,
  The Name of Christ our King;
Beneath His Cross we rally now
  And Hallelujah sing.

Tune Lochby—Missionary Hymnal, page 40.

in our fee - ble ef - forts proves His ten - derness, un - told.
we are sure from His dear word He saves the chil-dren still.
in your treas-ures as He brings The heath - en na - tions home.

Anon.

(*a*) 1 We come to ask our Father now
　　　That eyes be made to see
　　　And hearts to burn and lips to say,
　　　What can I give to Thee?

Cho.　We are a Foreign Mission Band
　　　With hearts right brave to do,
　　　We'll give to Jesus all we can
　　　And prove our hearts are true.

　　2 We know we're little and our store
　　　Of pennies is but small
　　　But then we want to bring e'en these,
　　　To God, who giveth all. Cho.

　　3 The older folks can give Thee more,
　　　Of work and money too,
　　　This night, O help them from their store,
　　　Their larger part to do. Cho.

(*b*) 4 Dear Lord, may what has now been given,
　　　Find some sweet work to do,
　　　Show some poor soul the way to heaven,
　　　And help us find it too. Cho.

(*a*) To be sung at collection time.
(*b*) After collection.

VOX ANGELICA.

F. W. FABER, 1849.

Rev. J. B. DYKES, 1868.

1. Hark! hark, my soul! an - gel - ic songs are swell - ing,
2. On - ward we go, for still we hear them sing - ing,
3. Far, far a - way, like bells at even - ing peal - ing,
4. An - gels, sing on! your faith - ful watch - es keep - ing,

O'er earth's green fields, and o - cean's wave - beat shore.
"Come, wea - ry souls, for Je - sus bids you come!"
The voice of Je - sus sounds o'er land and sea;
Sing us sweet frag - ments of the songs a - bove,

How sweet the truth those bless - ed strains are tell - ing,
And thro' the dark its ech - oes sweet - ly ring - ing,
And la - den souls by thou-sands meek - ly steal - ing,
Till morn - ing's joy shall end the night of weep - ing,

Of that new life when sin shall be no more.
The mus - ic of the Gos - pel leads us home.
Kind Shep - herd, turn their wea - ry steps to Thee.
And life's long shad - ows break in cloud - less love.

CHORUS.

An - gels of Je - sus, An - gels of light, Sing - ing to

wel - come the pil - grims of the night, Sing - ing to

wel - come the pil - grims, the pil - grims of the night.

EWING.

Lawrence Tuttiett, 1866.

Alexander Ewing, 1860.

1. Go for-ward, Christian sol - dier, Be-neath His ban - ner true;
2. Go for-ward, Christian sol - dier, Nor dream of peac - ful rest,
3. Go for-ward, Christian sol - dier, Fear not the gath-'ring night;

The Lord Him - self thy lead - er, Shall all thy foes sub - due.
Till Sa - tan's host is vanquished, And heav'n is all pos - sessed;
The Lord has been thy shel - ter, The Lord will be thy light;

His love fore - tells thy tri - als, He knows thine hour - ly need:
Till Christ Him - self shall call thee, To lay thine ar - mor by,
When morn His face re - veal - eth, Thy dan - gers all are past;

He   can   with bread of   hea - ven   Thy faint-ing   spir - it feed.
And wear   in   end-less   glo - ry   The crown of   vic - to - ry.
O   pray   that faith and   vir - tue   May keep thee   to   the last.

TUNE Ewing.

Dr. Rankin 1887.

1   Read o'er your marching orders,
   Sealed with your Leader's blood;
"To earth's remotest borders"
   Proclaim the Lamb of God!
Set life and death before them,
   The Jew, the Greek as well;
There is one Father o'er them
   Who doeth all things well.

2   Read o'er your marching orders!
   Who knows so well as He
The depths of sin's disorders,
   Its curse and misery?
There is but one salvation
   From sin and death and hell,
To every tribe and nation
   Let the sweet tidings swell.

3   Enough for you the mission,
   The gospel tale to tell,
Under the great commission
   That saves from death and hell.
Read o'er your marching orders,
   His flag must be unfurled
In earth's remotest borders;
   Must float all round the world!

Rev. JOHN MASON NEALE.   ARTHUR SEYMOUR SULLIVAN, 1872.

1. Come ye faith-ful, raise the strain, Of tri - um - phant
2. 'Tis the spring of souls to - day, Christ hath burst his
3. Now the Queen of sea - sons, bright With the day of
4. Al - le - lu - ia! now we cry, To our King im -

glad - ness! God hath bro't His Is - ra - el
pris - on, From the frost and gloom of death,
splen - dor, With the roy - al feast of feasts,
mor - tal, Who tri - um - phant burst the bars

In - to joy from sad - ness,— Loos'd from Pha - raoh's
Light and life have ris - en, All the win - ter
Comes its joy to ren - der Comes to glad Je -
Of the tomb's dark por - tal; Al - le - lu - ia,

bit - ter yoke, Ja - cob's sons and daugh - ters,
of our sins, Long and and dark is fly -
ru - sa - lem, Who with true af - fec - tion,
with the Son, God, the Fa - ther, prais - ing;

Led them with un-moist-'en'd feet Thro' the Red Sea wa - ters.
From His face to whom we give Thanks and praise un - dy - ing.
Wel-comes in un-wea-ried strains, Je - sus' res - ur - rec - tion.
Al - le - lu - ia! yet a - gain, To the Spir - it rais - ing.

Anon.

BAVARIA.
German.

1. Lord, her watch Thy church is keep - ing; When shall
2. Ti - dings send to ev - 'ry crea - ture, Mil - lions
3. Then the end! Thy church com - plet - ed, All Thy

earth Thy rule o - bey? When shall end the night of
yet have nev - er heard, Can they hear with - out a
chos - en gath-er'd in, With their King in glo - ry

weep - ing, When shall break the prom - ised day?
preach - er? Lord Al - might - y give the word!
seat - ed, Sa - tan bound, and ban - ished sin;

See the white-ning har-vest lan-guish, Wait-ing still the laborer's toil; Was it vain Thy Son's deep an-guish? Shall the strong re-tain the spoil?

Give the word! in ev-'ry na-tion! Let the gos-pel trumpet sound. Wit-ness-ing a world's sal-va-tion, To the earth's re-mot-est bound.

Gone for-ev-er, part-ing, weep-ing, Hun-ger sor-row, death and pain: Lo! her watch Thy church is keep-ing, Come, Lord Je-sus, come to reign

SAMUEL.

Rev. JAMES DRUMMOND BURNS, 1856.   ARTHUR SEYMOUR SULLIVAN, 1872.

1. Hushed was the eve - ning hymn, The tem - ple courts were dark:
2. The old man meek and mild, The priest of Is - rael, slept;
3. O! give me Sam - uel's ear, The o - pen ear, oh Lord,
4. O! give me Sam - uel's heart A low - ly heart that waits
5. O! give me Sam - uel's mind, A sweet un - murm'ring faith

The lamp was burn - ing dim, Be - fore the sa - cred Ark;
His watch the tem - ple child, The lit - tle Le - vite kept;
A - live and quick to hear Each whis - per of Thy word;
Where in Thy house Thou art, Or watch - es at Thy gates,
O - be - dient and re - sign'd To Thee in life And death;

When sud - den - ly a voice Di - vine Rang
And what from E - li's sense was seal'd, The
Like Him to an - swer at Thy call, And
By day and night; a heart that still Moves
That I may reach, with child - like eyes, Truths

through the si - lence at the shrine.
Lord to Han - nah's Son re - vealed.
to o - bey Thee, first of all.
at the breath - ing of Thy will.
that are hid - den from the wise. A - men.

Anon.

PASTORAL

1. Great Shep - herd of the sheep, Who all Thy flock dost
2. But when the road is long, Thy ten - der arm and
3. Till from the soil of sin, Cleans'd and made pure with -

keep, Lead - ing by wa - ters calm; Do
strong, The wea - ry one will bear; And
in, Dear Sav - ior, whose I am, Thou

Thou my foot - steps guide, To fol - low by Thy side; Make
Thou wilt wash me clean And lead to pas - tures green, Where
bring - est me in love, To Thy safe fold a - bove, A

me Thy lit - tle lamb, Make me Thy lit - tle Lamb.
all the flowers are fair, Where all the flow'rs are fair.
lit - tle snow-white lamb, A lit - tle snow - white lamb.

From Sunday School Hymnal by per.

HEAR US, HOLY JESUS.

1. Je - sus, from Thy throne on high, Far a-bove the bright blue sky,
2. Lit - tle chil dren need not fear, When they know that Thou art near,
3. Lit - tle hearts may love Thee well, Lit - tle lips Thy love may tell,
4. Lit - tle lives may be di - vine, Lit - tle deeds of love may shine,
5. May we prize our Chris-tian name, May we guard it free from blame,
6. May our tho'ts be un - de - filed, May our words be true and mild,

Look on us with lov - ing eye, *Hear us, Ho - ly Je - sus.*
Thou dost love us, Sav- ior dear, *Hear us, Ho - ly Je - sus.*
Lit - tle hymns Thy prais-es swell, *Hear us, Ho - ly Je - sus.*
Lit - tle ones be whol - ly Thine, *Hear us, Ho - ly Je - sus.*
Fear - ing all that caus - es shame, *Hear us, Ho - ly Je - sus.*
Make us each a ho - ly child, *Hear us, Ho - ly Je - sus.*

From the S. S. Hymnal. by per.

54

ANON.   REV. ROBERT LOWRY, by per.

1. Once a - gain the bells are ring-ing, Hearts and voi - ces join the
2. Once at midnight, cold and star - ry, Heaven's gates were o-pened
3. Oth - er doors the Sav - ior o-pened, And by ear - nest work and
4. Yes to lands so long in darkness, Where the chil-dren live in
5. Till in dis-tant lands and na-tions Ev - 'ry door shall o - pen

song, Peace and love, and glad thanks-giv - ing To our
wide, To the world, then lost in dark - ness, Came our
prayer, We must fol - low in His foot - steps, Strive to
sin, We must march with ban - ners fly - ing, For His
wide, And the chil - dren learn with glad - ness, The full

Christ - mas - tide ue - long. Peace and joy to heath-en
Je - sus to a - bide.
seek and en - ter there.
sake to en - ter in.
joy of Christ - mas - tide.

chil - dren, For Je - sus came to save in boundless love—

Came to earth that they might live for-ev-er In the Father's home a - bove.

RUTHERFORD.

Annie Ross Cousin, 1857.

Chas. D'Urhan, 1845.

1. The sands of time are sink - ing. The dawn of heav - en breaks; The
2. Oh! Christ He is the foun - tain, The deep, sweet well of love, The
3. Oh! I am my Be - lov - ed's, And my Be - lov - ed's mine, He

sum - mer morn I've sighed for, The fair, sweet morn a - wakes: Oh,
streams of earth I've tast - ed, More deep I'll drink a - bove; There,
brings a poor vile sin - ner, In - to His house di - vine, Up -

dark hath been the mid - night, But day-spring is at hand, And
to an o - cean full - ness, His mer - cy doth ex - pand, And
on The Rock of A - ges My soul redeem'd shall stand, When

glo - ry, glo - ry, dwell - eth, In Im - man-uel's land. A - men.

INSPRUCK.

Arr. by C. H. Rink.

O Spir - it of the liv - ing God, Help Thou Thy chil-dren;

1st.   2nd.   FINE.

send a - broad The Gos - pel of Thy grace.
And i - dol wor - - ship cease,

Till all mankind Thy love shall see, In Jesus' name, shall bow the knee,

58

ANDREW YOUNG, 1838.

SAM. SEBASTIAN WESLEY, 1864.

1. There is a hap - py land, Far, far a - way;
2. Come to that hap - py land, Come, come a - way;
3. Bright in that hap - py land, Beams ev - 'ry eye,

Where saints in glo - ry stand Bright, bright as day,
Why will ye doubt - ing stand, Why still de - lay?
Kept by a Fa - ther's hand, Love can - not die.

Oh, how they sweet - ly sing, Wor - thy is our Sav - ior King,
Oh, we shall hap - py be, When from sin and sor - row free;
Oh, then to glo - ry run, Be a crown and king - dom won;

OCEANA.

Florence E. Homer. Edward D. Eaton.

1. A - hoy, a - hoy, good ship, a - hoy! What craft is this we meet?
2. A - hoy, a - hoy, good ship, a - hoy! Who knows her har-bor homes?
3. A - hoy, a - hoy, good ship, a - hoy! Who knows the news she bears?

'Tis Je - sus' ship, Let ev - 'ry lip, That gos-pel ban-ner greet.
A mil- lion ports, In children's hearts, Stand wide for the day she comes.
'Tis Je - sus' love, She goes to prove, We follow her course with prayers.

Chorus.

Speed, speed, come shout a good speed, as fast she sails and far. Her

beau - ti - ful name is of heav-'nly fame, Our bless - ed Morning Star!

Moderato.

1. Lord of my life, whose ten - der care, Hath
2. O may I dai - ly, hour - ly, strive In
3. With pray'r, my hum - ble praise I bring, For

led me on till now, Here low - ly, at the
heav'n - ly grace to grow; To Thee and to Thy
mer - cies, day by day; Lord, teach my heart Thy

hour of pray'r, Be - fore Thy throne I bow; I bless Thy gra-cious
glo - ry, live, Dead to all else be - low; Tread in the path my
love to sing, Lord, teach me how to pray; All that I am, and

hand, and pray For - giv - ness for an - oth - er day.
Sav - ior trod, Tho' thorn - y, yet the path of God.
have, to Thee I of - fer through e - ter - ni - ty.

From the S. S. Hymnal. by per.

Mrs. Elizabeth Charles.　　　　Friedrich Ferdinand Flemming, 1810.

1. Praise ye the Fa - ther! for His lov - ing kind - ness,
2. Praise ye the Sav - ior! great is His com - pas - sion,
3. Praise ye the Spir - it! Com - fort - er of Is - rael,

Ten - der - ly cares He, for His err - ing chil - dren; Praise Him, ye
Gra - cious - ly cares He, for His chos - en peo - ple; Young men and
Sent of the Fa - ther and the Son to bless us; Praise ye the

an - gels, praise Him in the heav - ens, Praise ye, Je - ho - vah!
maid - ens, ye old men and chil - dren, Praise ye, the Sav - ior!
Fa - ther, Son and Ho - ly Spir - it, Praise ye, the Tri - une God!

ANON.

ST. HELIER.

1. The wise may bring their learn - ing, The rich may bring their
2. We'll bring Him hearts that love Him, We'll bring Him thank-ful
3. We bring the lit - tle du - ties We have to do each

wealth, And some may bring their great - ness, And
praise; And young souls meek - ly striv - ing To
day, We'll try our best to please Him, At

some bring strength and health; We, too, would bring our
walk in ho - ly ways, And these shall be the
home, at school, at play, And bet - ter are these

treas - ures, To of - fer to the King; We
treas - uses, We of - fer to our King, And
treas - ures, To of - fer to our King, Than

From S. S. Hymnal, by per.

have   no wealth or   learn - ing, What   shall   we   chil - dren   bring?
these   are gifts that   ev - er   The   poor - est   child   may   bring.
rich - est   gifts with - out   them; Yet these   a   child   may   bring.

O LAMB OF GOD

Quietly.

1. O   Lamb of   God most   low - ly!   All   free from spot and   stain,
2. O   Lamb of   God most   ho - ly!   So   great and   yet   so   meek,
2. O   Lamb of   God most   gen -tle!   So   kind and   good and   true;
4. O   Lamb of   God most   love - ly!   To   Thee   our   faith would   flee;

O   help   us   now to serve Thee, And   sing Thy praise a - gain.
May we when pride al-lures us,   Thy   low - ly   spir - it   seek.
May we when passion tempts us, Thy   gen - tle-ness   pur - sue.
Re-veal   to   us   Thy beau-ty, And   win our hearts to   Thee.   A - MEN.

From S. S. Hymnal, by per.

CLEMENT OF ALEXANDRI

Trans. by HENRY M. DEXTER, 1846.

FELICE GIARDINI, 1760.

1. Shep-herd, of ten - der youth, Guid-ing in love and trut
3. Lo! now and till we die, Sound we Thy praise on high

Thro' de - vious ways! Christ, our tri - um - phant King, We come Thy
And joy - ful sing! In - fants and all the throng, Who to Thy

name to sing, And here our chil - dren bring To shout Thy praise.
church be-long, U - nite to swell the song To Christ, our King

RUSSIAN FOLK SONG.

Anon.

1. In - to those far off lands We send the Joy - ful sound, And
2. In - to those dis - tant lands Which now in dark - ness dwell, We
3. Far o - ver all the lands We sow the Gos - pel grain, That

pray that its sweet ech - o there, May in each heart be found.
send the bless - ed heav'n - ly light, The shad - ows to dis - pel.
faith - ful hearts may flour - ish there When Je - sus comes to reign.

TUNE Russian Folk Song.

John Burton.

1 I have often said my prayers,
   But do I ever pray?
   And do the wishes of my heart
   Go with the words I say?

2 And I may as well kneel down
   To worship gods of stone,
   As offer to the living God
   A prayer of words alone.

3 For words without the heart
   The Lord will never hear,
   Nor will He to those lips attend,
   Whose prayers are not sincere.

WORGAN.

Trans. by Miss KATHERINE WINCKWORTH, 1858.

HENRY CAREY, 1708.

1. Christ, the Lord, is ris'n a - gain, Hal - - le - lu - jah!
2. He, who bore all pain and loss, Hal - - le - lu - jah!.
3. He, who slumber'd in the grave, Hal - - le - lu - jah!
4. Now He bids us tell a - broad, Hal - - le - lu - jah!
5. Thou, our Pas-chal Lamb in - deed, Hal - - le - lu - jah!

Christ hath brok-en ev - 'ry chain; Hal - - - le - lu - jah!
Com - fort-less up - on the cross, Hal - - - le - lu - jah!
Is ex - alt - ed now to save; Hal - - - le - lu - jah!
How the lost may be re - stored, Hal - - - le - lu - jah!
Christ, Thy ransomed peo-ple feed! Hal - - - le - lu - jah!

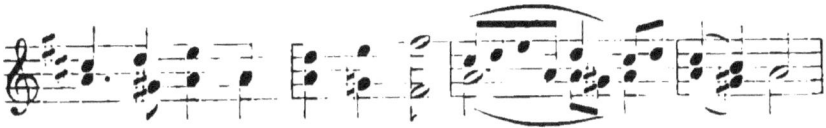

Hark! an-gel-ic voi-ces cry, Hal - - - le - lu - jah!
Lives in glo-ry now on high. Hal - - - le - lu - jah!
Now thro' Christen-dom it rings, Hal - - - le - lu - jah!
How the pen-i-tent for-giv'n, Hal - - - le - lu - jah!
Take our sins and guilt a-way, Hal - - - le - lu - jah!

Sing-ing ev-er-more on high, Hal - - le - lu - jah!
Pleads for us and hears our cry; Hal - - le - lu - jah!
That the Lamb is King of kings: Hal - - le - lu - jah!
How we too may en-ter heav'n: Hal - - le - lu - jah!
That we all may sing for aye, Hal - - le - lu - jah!

WATCHMAN. 7s, D.

John Bowring, 1825.

Lowell Mason, 1830.

1. Watch - man, tell us of the night, What its signs of
2. Watch - man, tell us of the night, High - er yet that
3. Watch - man, tell us of the night, For the morn - ing

prom - ise are? Trav' - ler, o'er yon moun - tain's height
star as - scends, Trav' - ler, bless - ed - ness and light,
seems to dawn; Trav' - ler, dark - ness takes its flight,

See that glo - ry beam - ing star! Watch - man, does its
Peace and truth its course por - tends; Watch - man, will its
Doubt and ter - ror are with-drawn; Watch - man, let thy

Trav'-ler, yes; it brings the day, Prom-ised day of Is - ra - el;
Trav'-ler, a - ges are its own, See it bursts o'er all the earth!
Trav'-ler, lo! the Prince of peace, Lo! the Son of God is come.

ANON.

COLTON,
B. C. F. 1887.

1. On - ly a drop in the buck-et, But ev - ery drop will tell; The
2. On - ly a poor little pen - ny, It was all I had to give, But as
3. God loveth the cheerful giv - er, Tho' the gift be poor and small; But

buck-et would soon be emp - ty, With-out the drops in the well.
pen - nies make the dol - lars, It may help the cause to live.
what must He think of His children, When they never give at all.

Copyright, on Music, 1887.

Dedicated to Young Ladies' Missionary Society
of Union Park Church, Chicago.

COME, HOLY SPIRIT.

Not too slowly.

1. Come, Ho - ly Spir - it, Power di - vine, Our wait - ing
2. Help us by low - ly lives and meek Thy power in

souls in - spire; Un - seal our lips, our hearts re-
us to show, That oth - er hearts Thy grace may

fine With touch of heav'n - ly fire. We have no
seek, And Thy sweet pres - ence know. Teach us to

Music from Sunday School Hymnal, by per. Words copyrighted, 1888.

wis - dom of our own, No strength to do Thy will;
pray thro' Christ our Lord; Bring sin - ful wan - d'rers home;

Come, make in ev - 'ry heart Thy throne, Thy prom - is -
Give tongues of flame to speak Thy Word: Come, Ho - ly

es ful - fill; Thy prom - is - es ful - fill.*
Spir - it, come; Come, Ho - ly Spir - it, come.

* Rev. 2: 26. And he that overcometh, and keepeth my works unto the end, to him will I give power over the nations: See also Rev. 2: 17.

ROSEDALE.

Dr. Bonar.

Geo. F. Root, 1839.

1. Go, la - bor on while it is day; The world's dark
2. Men die in dark - ness at your side, With - out a
3. Toil on, faint not, keep watch and pray! Be wise the
4. Go, la - bor on, your hands are weak; Your knees are

night is haste - ning on; Speed, speed your work, cast
hope to cheer the tomb; Take up the torch and
err - ing soul to win. Go forth in - to the
faint, your soul cast down; Yet fal - ter not, the

sloth a - way! It is not thus that souls are won.
wave it wide—The torch that lights time's thick - est gloom
world's high-way; Com - pel the wan - derer to come in.
prize you seek, Is near, a King - dom and a Crown.

CHRISTMAS.

NAHUM TATE.

GEO. FRED. HANDEL.

1. While shepherd's watch'd their flocks by night, All seat - ed
2. "Fear not," He said, for might - y dread Had seized their
3. "To you, in Da - vid's town this day, Is born of
4. "Tho heav'n - ly babe you there shall find, To hu - man
5. Thus spake the ser - aph, and forth -with Ap - peared a
6. All glo - ry be to God on high And to the

on the ground, The an - gel of the Lord came down,
trou - bled mind, "Glad ti - dings of great joy, I bring,
Da - vid's line, The Sav - ior, who is Christ, the Lord,
view dis - played, All mean -ly wrapp'd in swath - ing bands,
shin - ing throng, Of an - gels prais - ing God, who thus
earth be peace; Good- will, hence-forth from heav'n to men,

And glo - ry shone a - round, And glo - ry shone a-round.
To you and all man - kind, To you and all mankind."
And this shall be the sign, And this shall be the sign.
And in a man - ger laid, And in a man - ger laid."
Ad- dress'd their joy - ful song, Ad - dress'd their joy - ful song."
Be - gin and nev - er cease, Be - gin and nev - er cease.

A SONG PRAYER.

Written for Children's Day at the Church
of the Redeemer, Lake View, Ills,

Rev. W. A. BARTLETT.

Spirited.

1. Je - sus hear us as we pray, In this song on Chil-dren
2. Thou hast kept us in Thy way, Watch-ing lest our feet shou
3. Guard our friends with ten-der care; Bless and keep them ev - 'ry
4. Like the flow - ers may we be, Bright and fra - grant lives for

In the

Day; May our love en-rich our voic - es, In the
stray; And we thank Thee for Thy mer - cy, Which has
where When the shad - ows fall a - round them, Send, oh
Thee; And, when this brief life is o - ver, Call us

praise we bring to

CHORUS.

praise we bring, we bring to Thee. Ho - ly Fa - ther. We Thy
brought us, brought us thro' the year.
send, oh send, Thy light to cheer.
home, us home to dwell on high.

Copyright on Words and Music, 1897.

Hum - bly bring........ our songs to
chil - dren Hum - bly bring our song to Thee, we
Hum - bly bring our song our song to

Thee,...... Wilt Thou
bring our song to Thee; Wilt Thou bless, ac - cept, for - give and
Thee,...... Wilt Thou

love us, In the Sav - ior's name we pray.

THANK OFFERING HYMN.

Mrs. Myra Pitkin.

1. Bring gifts un - to the Lord to - day, From
2. We thank Him for His lov - ing care, Of
3. We thank Him that His love has stirred, The
4. And for our - selves, each heart can tell Of
5. Shall we then take His gifts so free, And
6. Nay! our thank - off - 'rings let us bring, And

grate - ful hearts let praise as - cend To Him whose mer - cy
those who toil in heath - en lands, We give our gold, our
hearts of ma - ny heath - en born, To spread a - broad His
an - swered prayer, of paths made plain, Of light in dark - ness
give Him nought but word of praise, What of - fer - ing too
on His al - tar lay them down, And may our glo - rious

crowns our way, With good we scarce can com - pre - hend.
love, our prayer, But He has hol - den up their hands.
sav - ing word, And res - cue oth - ers still for - lorn.
peace that fell Like dew on spir - its spent with pain.
great could be For love that so hath crowned our days,
Sav - ior King, Our praise, with His ac - cept - ance, crown

Music by permission of S. S. Hymnal.

WESLEY.

Thomas Hastings, 1830.

Lowell Mason, 1830.

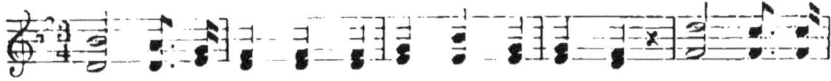

1. Hail, to the brightness of Zi - on's glad morning! Joy to the
2. Hail, to the brightness of Zi - on's glad morning! Long by the
3. Lo! in the des - ert, rich flow - ers are springing; Streams ev - er
4. See, from all lands, from the isle of the o - cean, Praise to Je -

lands that in dark-ness have lain! Hush'd be the ac - cents of
proph - ets of Is - rael fore - told; Hail to the mil - lions from
co - pious are glid- ing a - long; Loud from the moun-tain tops
ho - vah as - cend-ing on high; Fall'n are the en - gines of

sor-row and mourning; Zi - on in tri-umph be - gins her mild reign.
bond-age re - turn - ing, Gen - tiles and Jews the blest vi - sion be - hold.
ech - oes are ring - ing; Wastes rise in ver-dure, and min-gle in song.
war and com - mo - tion; Shouts of Sal - va - tion are rend-ing the sky.

ST. SYLVESTER.

Louise M. Alcott, by per.

Rev. John Bacchus Dykes, 1861.

1. What shall little children bring,
2. Gathered in a happy fold,
3. Sheltered by protecting arms,
4. Willing hearts and open hands,

As a grateful offering, For the ever watch-
Safe from wintry want and cold, Fed by hands that nev-
From the great world's sins and harms, While a patience wise
Love that ev - 'ry ill withstands, Faith and hope in Thee

ful care, That surrounds us ev 'ry where.
er tire, Warmed by loves unfailing fire.
and sweet, Guides our little wan-d'ring feet.
our King, These shall be our offering.

Mary Mapes Dodge, by per.   Samuel Weber.

1. Can a lit-tle child like me, Thank the Fa-ther fit-ing-ly?
2. For the fruit up-on the tree, For the birds that sing of Thee,

Yes, oh yes, be good and true, Patient, kind in all you do,
For the earth, in beau-ty drest Father, moth-er and the rest;

Love the Lord and do your part, Learn to say with all your heart,
For thy pre-cious lov-ing care, For Thy boun-ty ev-'ry where,

SARAH FLOWER ADAMS, 1840.

SIR ARTHUR SULLIVAN, 1872.

1. Near - er, my God, to Thee, Near - er to Thee,
2. Tho' like a wan - der - er, The sun gone down,
3. There let the way ap - pear, Steps un - to heaven;
4. Then, with my wak - ing thoughts, Bright with Thy praise,
5. Or if, on joy - ful wing Cleav - ing the sky,

E'en tho' it be a cross That rais - eth me.
Dark - ness be o - ver me, My rest a stone,
All that Thou send - est me In mer - cy given:
Out of my ston - y griefs Beth - el I'll raise;
Sun, moon, and stars for - got, Up - ward I fly,

Still all my song shall be, Near - er my God to Thee,
Yet in my dreams I'd be, Near' - er my God to Thee,
An - gels to beck - on me, Near - er my God to Thee,
So by my woes to be, Near - er my God to Thee,
Still all my song shall be, Near - er my God to Thee,

Near - er, my God, to Thee, Near - er to Thee.

THATCHER.

R. WARDLAW.

GEO. FREDERIC HANDEL, 1732.

1. O Lord, our God, a - rise! The cause of
2. Thou Prince of life, a - rise! Nor let Thy
3. Thou Ho - ly Ghost, a - rise! Ex - tend Thy

truth main - tain; And wide o'er all the peo - pled
glo - ry cease; Far spread the con - quests of Thy
heal - ing wing, And o'er a dark and ru - ined

world Ex - tend her bless - ed reign.
grace, And bless the earth with peace.
world Let light and or - der spring.

Mrs. Elizabeth Payson Prentiss, 1869.　　　　William Howard Doane.

1. More love to Thee O Christ, More love to Thee;　Hear Thou the
2. Once earth-ly joy I craved, Sought peace and rest;　Now Thee a
3. Let sor-row do its work, Send grief and pain;　Sweet are Thy
4. Then shall my lat - est breath Whis - per Thy praise;　This be the

prayer I make On bend- ed knee; This is my earn-est plea,
lone I seek, Give what is best, This all my pray'r shall be,
mes - sen - gers, Sweet their re - frain, When they can sing with me,
part - ing cry, My heart shall raise, This still its prayer shall be,

More love, O Christ, to Thee, More love to Thee, More love to Thee!

Music by permission of Biglow & Main.

GLAD TIDINGS.

W. A. MUHLENBURG, 1826.

CHARLES AVISON.

1 Shout the glad tid - ings, ex - ult - ing - ly sing; Je -
2. Shout the glad tid - ings, ex - ult - ing - ly sing; Je -
3. Shout the glad tid - ings, ex - ult - ing - ly sing; Je -

ru - sa - lem triumphs, Mes - si - ah is King! Zi - on, the
ru - sa - lem triumphs, Mes - si - ah is King! Tell how He
ru - sa - lem triumphs, Mes - si - ah is King! Mor-tals, your

mar - vel - ous sto - ry be tell - ing, The Son of the
com - eth from na - tion, to na - tion, The heart-cheer-ing
hom - age be grate - ful - ly bring-ing, And sweet let the

High - est, how low - ly His birth! The bright - est arch -
news, let the earth ech - o round, How free to the
glad - some ho - san - na a - rise; Ye an - gels, the

an - gel in glo - ry ex - cell - ing, He stoops to re -
faith - ful He of - fers sal - va - tion. How His peo - ple with
full hal - le - lu - jah be sing - ing, One cho - rus re -

deem thee, He reigns up - on earth. Shout the glad
joy ev - er - last - ing are crown'd. Shout the glad
sound thro' the earth and the skies. Shout the glad

tid - ings, ex - ult - ing - ly sing; ... Je - ru - sa - lem triumphs, Mes -

si - ah is King! Mes - si - ah is King! Mes - si - ah is King!

86

JAMES EDMESTON, 1822.   Rev. J. S. SIDEBOTHAM.

1. When shall the voice of sing - ing Flow joy - ful - ly a - long? When
2. Then from the crag-gy moun-tains The sa-cred shout shall fly, And

hill and val - ley ring - ing With one tri - um-phant song, Pro-
sha - dy vales and fount-ains Shall ech - o the re - ply: High

claim the con - test end - ed, And Him who once was slain A -
tower and low - ly dwell-ing, Shall send the cho - rus round, All

gain to earth de - scend - ed, In right - eous-ness to reign.
Hal - le - lu jahs swell - ing, In one e - ter-nal sound.

LUELLA.

Anon.

HENRY N. WHITNEY.

1. Je - sus, ten - der Sav - ior, Hast Thou died for me?
2. Now I know Thou lov - est, And dost plead for me?

Make me ver - y thank - ful, In my heart to Thee.
Make me ver - y thank - ful, In my prayers to Thee.

When the sad, sad sto - ry Of Thy grief I read,
Soon I hope in glo - ry At Thy side to stand,

Make me ver - y sor - ry, For my sins in - deed.
Make me fit to meet Thee, In that hap - py land.

ORIENT.

BISHOP HEBER. 1811.

MOZART.

1. Brightest and best of the sons of the morn-ing, Dawn on our
2. Cold on His cra - dle the dewdrops are shin - ing, Low lies His
3. Say, shall we yield Him in cost - ly de - vo - tions, O - dors of
4. Vain - ly we of - fer each am - ple ob - la - tion, Vain - ly with

dark - ness and lend us Thine aid, Star of the East the ho -
head with the beast of the stall, An - gels a - dore Him in
E - dom and of-f'rings di - vine, Gems of the moun-tain and
gifts would His fa - vor se - cure: Rich - er by far is the

ri - zon a-dorn ing, Guide where our in-fant Re - deem-er is laid.
slumber re - clin - ing, Mak-er and Monarch and Sav - ior of all.
pearls of the o-cean, Myrrh from the for - est, or gold from the mine.
heart's ad - o - ra - tion: Dearer to God are the prayers of the poor.

SAFE HOME.

Rev. Robt. Moffat.   Sir Arthur Sullivan, 1872.

1. Can I, a lit - tle child, Do a - ny-thing for those Who are by sin de -
2. First then I would implore The Lord to change each heart, Then from my lit-tle
3. How would such joy-ful news Their inmost souls delight, And who would then re-

filed, To light en their sad woes. I can - not see the
store I free - ly will im - part, That some kind teach-ers
fuse To give his lit - tle mite, That ev - ery heath-en

rea - son why I may not if I real - ly try.
may be given To point out Christ, the way to heav'n.
child may know The bless - ings Je - sus can be - stow.

LUCIUS.

Mrs. K. H. Johnson, 1873. by per.

Fred. L. Morey.

1. The whole wide world for Je - sus, Once more be - fore we part,
2. The whole wide world for Je - sus, From out the Gol-den gate,
3. The whole wide world for Je - sus, Its hearts and homes and thrones;

Ring out the joy-ful watch-word, From ev - ery grateful heart.
Thro' all the South Sea is - lands, To China's princely state:
Ring out a - gain the watch-word In loud and joy - ous tones;

The whole wide world for Je - sus: Be this our bat - tle cry,
From In - dia's vales and mountains, Thro' Per-sia's land of bloom,
The whole wide world for Je - sus, With prayer the song we'll wing,

The cru - ci - fied shall con - quer, The vic - to - ry is nigh.
To sto - ried-Pal - es - ti - na And Af - ric's des - ert gloom.
And speed the prayer with la - bor Till earth shall crown Him King.

Copyright on Music, 1887.

ALL SAINTS.

REGINALD HEBER, 1827.   HENRY STEPHENS CUTLER, by per.

1. The Son of God goes forth to war, A king-ly crown to gain,   His
2. A no-ble ar-my, men and boys, The ma-tron and the maid,   A -

blood-red ban-ner streams a-far; Who follows in His train? Who
round the Sav-ior's throne re-joice, In robes of light ar-rayed. They

best can drink his cup of woe, Tri-um-phant o-ver pain,   Who
climbed the steep as-cent of heav'n Thro' peril, toil and pain: O

pa-tient bears His cross be-low, He fol-lows in His train.
God, to us may grace be given To fol-low in their train.

AURELIA.

ANON.   SAM. SEBASTIAN WESLEY, 1868.

1. There comes a wail of an - guish A - cross the o - cean wave,
2. We have the bless - ed gos - pel, We know its priceless worth,
3. Go plant the cross of Je - sus On each be-nighted shore,

It pleads for help, O, Chris - tians, Poor, dy - ing souls to save.
We read the grand old sto - ry Of Christ the Sav - ior's birth.
Go wave the gos - pel ban - ner, Till dark-ness reigns no more;

Those far off hea-then na - tions, Who sit in dark - est night,
O haste, ye faith - ful work - ers! To them the tid - ings bear,
And while the seed you scat - ter, Far o'er the o-cean's foam,

Now stretch their hands im - plor - ing, And cry to us for light.
Glad tid - ings of sal - va - tion, That they our light may share.
We'll pray for you and la - bor In mis - sion fields at home.

TUNE "Aurelia"

ANON.

1 The echo still is ringing
    The grey old earth around,
  The name of Jesus singing,
    With fuller, sweeter sound.
  From lands of date and palm tree,
    The glad young voices sing
  Hosanna in the highest,
    Hosanna to our King!

2 We, too, would join the triumph,
    We, too, would raise the song,
  Would swell the mighty chorus
    Of the adoring throng.
  For since He died to save us,
    Our hearts to Him we'll bring
  And follow Him forever.
    Jesus, the children's King.

TUNE, "Aurelia."

MRS. MARIA FRANCES ANDERSON.

1 Our country's voice is pleading,
    Ye men of God, arise!
  His providence is leading,
    The land before you lies;
  Day-gleams are o'er it brightening,
    And promise clothes the soil;
  Wide fields for harvest whitening,
    Invite the reaper's toil.

2 Go, where the waves are breaking
    On California's shore,
  Christ's precious gospel taking,
    More rich than golden ore;
  On Alleghany's mountains,
    Through all the western vale,
  Beside Missouri's fountains,
    Rehearse the wondrous tale.

3 The love of Christ unfolding,
    Speed on from east to west,
  Till all His cross beholding,
    In Him are fully blest.
  Great Author of salvation,
    Haste, haste the glorious day,
  When we, a ransomed nation,
    Thy sceptre shall obey.

94

SPANISH HYMN.

Anon.

1. Lit - tle build - ers all are we, Build - ers for e -
2. One by one the stones we lay, Build - ing slow - ly,
3. On mount Leb - a - non's fair heights, By our man - y

ter - ni - ty; Chil - dren of the Mis - sion Bands,
day by day, Build - ing for our love are we,
gath - ered mites, Where the Nile's sweet wa - ters pour;

Work - ing with our hearts and hands Build - ing tem - ples
In the lands be - yond the sea: Build - ing by each
Build - ing all the wide world o'er, And one day our

for our King, By the of - fer - ings we bring;
thought and pray'r For the souls that suf - fer there,
eyes shall see, In a glad e - ter - ni ty,

Liv - ing tem - ples He doth raise, Fill'd with life and light and praise.
Build - ing in the Hin-doo land, Where the i - dols are as sand.
"Liv - ing stones" we helped to bring, For the pal - ace of our King.

Anon.   Sir Arthur Sullivan.

1. Dear Sav - ior, bless the chil - dren Who've
2. Dear Lord, come Thou to help us, O -
3. Lord, bless the work we're do - - ing, And

gath - ered here to - day, O send thy Ho - ly
bey Thy great com - mand, And send the bless - ed
bless our gifts, though small, And hear our prayer for

Spir - it And teach us how to pray.
gos - pel A - broad thro' ev - ery land.
Je - sus' sake Who died to save us all.

HOLLINGSIDE.

C. WESLEY, 1740.

Rev. J. B. DYKES, 1861.

1. Je - sus, Lov - er of my soul, Let me to Thy
2. Oth - er ref - uge have I none, Hangs my help - less
3. Thou, O Christ, art all I want; More than all in
4. Plen -teous grace with Thee is found, Grace to par - don

bo - som fly, While the wa - ters near - er roll,
soul on Thee; Leave, ah! leave me not a - lone,
Thee I find; Raise the fall - en cheer the faint,
all my sin; Let the heal - ing streams a - bound.

While the tem - pest still is high. Hide me, O my
Still sup - port, and com - fort me! All my trust on
Heal the sick, and lead the blind. Just, and ho - ly
Make and keep me pure with - in; Thou of life the

Sav - ior! hide, Till the storm of life is past;
Thee is stayed, All my help from Thee I bring
is Thy name; I am all un - right - eous - ness;
Foun - tain art; Free - ly let me take of Thee;

Safe in - to the ha - ven guide, O, re - ceive my soul at last!
Cov - er my de - fence-less head, With the shad - ow of Thy wing.
Vile and full of sin I am, Thou art full of truth and grace.
Spring Thou up with - in my heart, Rise to all e - ter - ni - ty.

98

Mrs. Cecil Frances Alexander, 1848.　　　Richard Storrs Willis, 1860.

1. There is a green hill, far a - way, With
2. He died that we might be for - given, He
3. O dear - ly, dear - ly, has He loved, And

out a cit - y wall, Where the dear Lord was
died to make us good; That we might go at
we must love him too, And trust in His re -

cru - ci - fied, Who died to save us all.
last to heav'n, Saved by His pre - cious blood;
deem - ing blood, And try His works to do,

We may not know, we can - not tell, What
There was no oth - er good e - nough, To
For there's a green hill far a - way, With -

pains He had to bear, But we be - lieve it
pay the price of sin, He on - ly could un -
out a cit - y wall, Where the dear Lord was

was for us, He hung and suf - fered there.
lock the gate Of heav'n and let us in.
cru - ci - fied, Who died to save us all.

ST. SYLVESTER.

ANON.

REV. JOHN BACCHUS DYKE, 1861.

1. Hark! the sound of an - gel voi - ces
2. See, ce - les - tial ra - diance stream - ing,
3. West - ward all a - long the a - ges,
4. An - gels from the realms of glo - ry

O - ver Bethlehem's star - lit plain, Hark! the heav'nly host re -
Light-ing up the mid-night sky, 'Tis the promised Day-Star
Trace its path-way clear and bright, Star of hope to east-ern
Peace on earth de-light to sing, Chil-dren, tell the wondrous

joic - es, Je - sus comes on earth to reign.
gleam - ing, 'Tis the Day-Spring from on high.
sa - ges, Ra - diant now with gos - pel light.
sto - ry, Go, proclaim the Sa - vior King.

Mrs. ANNIE H. SHEPHERD, 1841. HENRY E. MATHEWS, 1854.

1. A-round the throne of God in heav'n, Ten thousand children stand;
2. What bro't them to that world a - bove, That heav'n so bright and fair;
3. Be-cause the Sav - ior shed His blood, To wash a - way their sin;
4. On earth they sought the Savior's grace, On earth they loved His name,

Chil- dren whose sins are all forgiven, A ho - ly, hap-py band,
Where all is peace and joy, and love; How came those children there?
Bathed in that pure and pre-cious flood, Be-hold them white and clean,
So now they see His bless-ed face, And stand be - fore the Lamb,

Sing-ing glo - ry, glo - ry, Glo-ry be to God on high.

FRANCES RIDLEY HAVERGAL.   ALBERTO RANDEGGER.

Quietly.

1. God   of   heav - en! hear our   sing - ing; On - ly
2. Let   Thy   King - dom come, we   pray Thee, Let   the
3. Let   the sweet and joy - ful sto - ry   Of   the
4. Fa - ther, send   the glo - rious hour,   Ev - 'ry

lit - tle ones are we, Yet a great pe - ti - tion
world in Thee find rest; Let all know Thee and o -
Sav - ior's won - drous love, Wake on earth a song of
heart be Thine a - lone! For the King - dom and the

bringing, Fa - ther, now we come to Thee.
bey Thee, Lov - ing, praising, blessing, blessed.
glo - ry, Like the an-gels' song a - bove.
pow'-er, And the glo - ry are Thine own.

104

DANIEL MARCH, 1869.

MOZART.

1. Hark! the voice of Je - sus say - ing "Who will go and
2. If you can - not cross the o - cean, And the heathen
3. If a-mong the old - er peo - ple You may not be
4. Let none hear you i - dly say - ing, "There is no-thing

work to - day, Fields are white, and har - vest wait - ing,
lands ex - plore, You can find the hea - then near - er,
apt to teach, "Feed my lambs," said Christ, our Shepherd,
I can do," While the souls of men are dy - ing,

Who will bear the sheaves a - way?" Loud and strong the
You can help them at your door. If you can - not
"Place the food with - in their reach," And it may be
And the Mas - ter calls for you. Take the task He

Mas - ter call - eth, Rich re-wards He of - fers thee,
give your thousands You can give the wid - ow's mite,
that the chil-dren, You have led with tremb - ling hand
gives you glad - ly, Let His work your pleas - ure be,

Who will an-swer glad - ly say - ing, "Here am I, send me, send me."
And the least you do for Je - sus Will be pre - cious in His sight.
Will be found a-mong your jew - els, When you reach the bet - ter land.
An-swer quickly when He call-eth, "Here am I, send me, send me."

TUNE, "Ellesdie."

Mrs. LYDIA H. SIGOURNEY.

1 Onward, onward men of heaven!
 Bear the gospel's banner high;
Rest not till its light is given,
 Star of every pagan sky:
Send it where the pilgrim stranger
 Faints beneath the torrid ray;
Bid the red-browed forest ranger
 Hail it, ere he fades away.

2 Rude in speech, or grim in feature,
 Dark in spirit though he be,
Show that light to every creature,—
 Prince or vassal, bond or free.
Lo! they haste to every nation,
 Host on host the ranks supply;
Onward! Christ is your salvation,
 And your death is victory.

R. M. EDWARDS.

German.

1. God make my life a lit - tle light, With
2. God make my life a lit - tle staff, Where -

in the world to glow, A lit - tle flame that
on the weak may rest, That so, what breath and

shin - eth bright Wher - ev - er I may go.
strength I have, May serve my neigh - bor best.

God make my life a lit - tle flower; That
God make my life a lit - tle hymn; Of

giv - eth joy to all, Con - tent to bloom in
ten - der-ness and praise, Of faith that nev - er

na - tive bower, Al - though its place be small.
wax - eth dim, In all His won - drous ways.

108

W. W. How, 1854.

WINGATE,

FRED. L. MOREY.

1. We give Thee but Thine own, What-e'er the gift may be, For
2. Oh, hearts are bruised and dead, And homes are bare and cold, And
3. To com-fort and to bless, To find a balm for woe, To
4. The cap-tive to re - lease, To God the lost to bring, To
5. And we believe Thy word, Tho' dim our faith may be; What-

all we have is Thine a - lone, A trust, O Lord, from Thee.
lambs, for whom the Shep - herd bled, Are stray - ing from the fold.
tend the lone and fa - ther - less, Is an - gels' work be - low.
teach the way of life and peace, It is a Christ-like thing.
e'er for Thine we do O Lord, We do it un - to Thee.

Rev. Gerard Moultrie, 1867.

Joseph Barnby, 1869.

1. We march, we march to vic - to - ry, With the

cross of the Lord be - fore us; With His lov - ing eye look-ing

down from the sky, And His ho - ly arm spread

Fine for 1st 2d & 3d v. Last verse only.

o'er us, His ho - ly arm spread o'er us, o'er us.

1. We come in the might of the Lord of Light,
2. Our sword is the Spir - it of God on High,
3. And the choir of an - gels with song a - waits
4. Then on - ward we march, our arms to prove,

A joy - ful host to meet Him; And we
Our hel - met His sal - va - tion, Our
Our march to the gold - en Si - on, For our
With the banner of Christ be - fore us, With His

put   to   flight   the   ar - mies of   night, That the
banner   the   Cross   of   Cal - va - ry,   Our
Captain   hath   bro - ken the   bra - zen gates, And
eye   of   love   look-ing down from a - bove, And His

sons   of   the   day   may   greet   Him,   The
watch - word, the   In   car - na - tion,   Our
burst   the   bars   of   ir - on,   And
Ho - - ly   Arm   spread o'er   us,   His

D. S.

sons   of   the   day   may   greet   Him   We
watch- word,   the   In - car - na - tion.   We
burst   the   bars   of   ir - on.   We
Ho - ly   Arm   spread o'er   us.   We

112

HASTINGS.

C. F. ALEXANDER.

FRED. L. MOREY.

1. Souls in hea - then dark-ness ly - ing, Where no light has
2. Christians, heark -en! none has taught them Of His love so
3. Haste, O! haste and spread the tid - ings, Wide to earth's re -
4. Lo! the hills for har-vest whit - en, All a - long each

bro - ken through, Souls that Je - sus bought by dy - ing,
deep and dear; Of the pre - cious price that bought them,
mot - est strand; Let no broth-er's bit - ter chid - ings,
dis - tant shore; Sea - ward far the is - lands bright - en;

Whom His soul in trav - ail knew; Thou sand voi - ces,
Of the nail, the thorn, the spear, Ye, who know Him,
Rise a - gainst us when we stand In the judg - ment
Light of na - tions, lead us o'er; When we seek them,

Copyright on Music, 1887, by W. B. M. I.

Thou-sand voi - ces Call us o'er the wa - ter blue.
Ye, who know Him, Guide them from their dark-ness drear.
In the judg-ment, From some far for - got - ten land.
When we seek them, Let Thy Spir - it go be - fore.

TUNE, "Lochby,"
Page 40.

Rev. E. H. Sears, 1850.

1 It came upon the midnight clear,
    That glorious song of old,
  From angels bending near the earth
    To touch their harps of gold;
  "Peace on the earth, good will to men
    From heaven's all glorious King,
  The world in solemn stillness lay
    To hear the angels sing."

2 Still through the cloven skies they come,
    With peaceful wings unfurled,
  And still their heavenly music floats
    O'er all the weary world;
  Above the sad and lowly plains
    They bend on hovering wing,
  And ever o'er its Babel-sounds,
    The blessed angels sing.

3 For lo! the days are hastening on,
    By prophet bards foretold,
  When with the ever-circling years
    Comes round the age of gold;
  When peace shall over all the earth
    Its ancient splendors fling.
  And the whole world give back the song,
    Which now the angels sing.

MARY. J. WILLCOX.

MORNING STAR HYMN.

1. O Morn - ing Star! Dear Morn - ing Star! May an - gels guard thy
2. Where dis - tant isl - ands wait to see God's law of love and
3. Who share thy cab - in home to-day? Who rule thy deck and

track a - far, And may love's clear and ho - ly light Shine
lib - er - ty, The Star, the Star, on shin - ing course, Comes
guide thy way? God bless and keep them ev - 'ry one, While

on thy path - way day and night. From isle to isle thy
like a beam from Christ's dear cross, To light their dark - ness,
soft winds waft them safe - ly on. In faith and love we

white wings fly To bear a mes - sage from on high,
heal their sin, Make "home, sweet home," where hate has been,
chil - dren gave Our gifts to launch thee on the wave.

Tell - ing on earth's re - mo - test shore,
And bring to ev - - 'ry trou - bled soul,
Our gifts and pray'rs thy way shall wing,

The sweet old sto - - ry o'er and o'er.
God's peace that mak - - eth pure and whole.
Till ev - 'ry isle crown Je - sus King.

116

IOWA.

Rev. Chas, Wesley, 1762.   Aaron Chapin, 1823.

1. A charge to keep I have, A God to
2. To serve the pres - ent age, My call ing
3. Arm me with jeal - ous care, As in Thy
4. Help me to watch and pray; And on Thy -

glo - ri - fy; A nev - er - dy ing
to ful fill; O may it all my
sight to live; And O, thy ser - vant,
- self re ly, As - sured, if I my

soul to save, And fit it for the sky.
powers en - gage, To do my Mas - ter's will.
Lord, pre - pare A strict ac - ' count to give.
trust be - tray, I shall for - ev - er die.

BISHOP DOANE, 1824.
JOHN BAPTISTE CALKIN, 1872.

1. Up - lift the ban - ner! Let it float Sky
2. Up - lift the ban - ner! Hea - then lands Shall
3. Up - lift the ban - ner! Let it float Sky
4. Up - lift the ban - ner! Wide and high, Sea

ward and sea - ward, high and wide; The sun shall light its
see from far the glo - rious sight, And na - tions, gathering
- ward and sea - ward, high and wide; Our glo - ry on - ly
ward and sky - ward let it shine: Nor skill, nor might, nor

shin - ing folds, The Cross on which the Sav - ior died.
at the call, Their spir - its kin - dle in its light.
in the Cross, Our on - ly hope, the Cru - ci - fied.
mer - it ours; We con - quer on - ly in that sign.

118

BOST

Anon.

1. Hark! the voi - ces loud - ly call - ing, Waft-ed hith - er
2. Hea-then moth - ers bow - ing blind - ly Un - to gods of

o'er the sea, And in tones en - treat - ing, ten - der,
wood and stone, By their cries and tears they call thee,

E - ven now they sum - mon thee. Call - ing, call - ing,
Now to make the Sav - ior known.

ev - er call - ing, Hark! the mes - sage is to thee.

From the S. S. Hymnal, by per.

Call-ing, call-ing, ev-er call-ing, Hark! the mes-sage is to thee.

TUNE, "Bost."

Anon.

1 Blessed Savior, Thou didst suffer
   Little ones to come to Thee,
Lo! we offer now our tribute,
   Let our praise accepted be;
Mid the hallelujahs ringing,
   Mid the burst of angel song
Stoop to hear our childish singing
   Listen to an infant throng.

2 For a cry of deepest sorrow,
   Comes across the waters blue;
"Ye who know salvation's story,
   Haste to help and save us too.
Shed, oh, shed the gospel glory
   O'er the darkness of our night,
Till the gloomy shadows vanish
   In its full and blessed light."

3 For the poor benighted millions
   We can give and work and pray,
And our gifts and prayers united,
   Sure will speed that happy day,
When no more to idols bowing
   All shall own our Jesus, King,
And ten thousand voices ringing
   Shall His praise victorious sing.

HERALD ANGELS.

Miss HARRIET AUBER, 1829.

FELIX MENDELSSOHN, 1846.

1. Has-ten, Lord, the glo-rious time, When beneath Mes-si-ah's sway,
2. Then shall wars and tu-mults cease, Then be ban-ish'd grief and pain;

Ev-'ry na-tion, ev-'ry clime, Shall the gos-pel call o-bey.
Right-eous-ness, and joy and peace, Un-dis-turb'd, shall ev-er reign.

Mightiest kings His power shall own, Heathen tribes His name a-dore;
Time shall sun and moon ob-scure, Seas be dried and rocks be riven;

Sa-tan and his host o'er-thrown, Bound in chains shall hurt no more,
But His reign shall still en-dure, End-less as the days of heaven,

Sa-tan and his host o'er-thrown, Bound in chains, shall hurt no more.
But his reign shall still en-dure, End-less as the days of heav'n.

TUNE, "Herald Angels."

Joshua Marsden, 1812

1 Go, ye messengers of God,
 Like the beams of morning fly;
Take the wonder working rod,
 Wave the banner cross on high:
Where the lofty minaret
 Gleams along the morning skies
Wave it till the crescent set,
 And the "Star of Jacob" rise.

2 Go to many a tropic isle
 In the bosom of the deep,
Where the skies forever smile,
 And th'oppressed forever weep.
O'er the negro's night of care
 Pour the living light of heaven.
Chase away the fiend despair
 Bid him hope to be forgiven.

3 Where the golden gates of day
 Open on the palmy East,
Wide the bleeding cross display,
 Spread the gospel's richest feast.
Bear the tidings round the ball,
 Visit every soil and sea,
Preach the cross of Christ to all,
 Christ, whose love is full and free.

122

CORONATION.

Rev. Edward Perronett, 1780.

Oliver Holden, 1793.

1. All hail, the pow'r of Je - sus' name! Let an - gels pros-trate
2. Ye cho - sen seed of Is - rael's race, Ye ran-som'd from the
3. Let ev - 'ry kin - dred, ev - 'ry tribe, On this ter - res - trial
4. Oh! that with yon - der sa -cred throng, We at His feet may

fall; Bring forth the roy - al di - a - dem, And
fall, Hail Him, who saves you by His grace, And
ball, To Him all maj - es - ty as - cribe, And
fall; We'll join the ev - er - last - ing song, And

crown Him Lord of all, Bring forth the roy - al
crown Him Lord of all, Hail Him who saves you
crown Him Lord of all, To Him all maj - es -
crown Him Lord of all, We'll join the ev - er -

di - a - dem, and crown Him Lord of all.
by His grace, and crown Him Lord of all.
ty as - cribe, and crown Him Lord of all.
last - ing song, and crown Him Lord of all.

TUNE, "Coronation.

ANON.

1 Hosanna! be the children's song
    To Christ, the children's King,
    His praise to whom our souls belong
    Let all the children sing.

2 Hosanna! on the wings of light,
    O'er earth and ocean fly,
    Till morn to eve, and noon to night
    And heaven to earth reply.

3 Hosanna! then our song shall be;
    Hosanna to our King,
    This is the children's jubilee,
    Let all the children sing.

Dorothy Ann Thrupp.   John H. Willcox.

1. Sav - ior, like a Shep -herd lead us, Much we need Thy
2. Thou hast promised to re - ceive us, Poor and sin - ful
3. Ear - ly let us seek Thy fa - vor, Ear - ly let us

ten - der care; In Thy pleas - ant pas - tures feed us;
tho' we be; Thou hast mer - cy to re - lieve us;
learn Thy will; Do Thou, Lord, our on - ly Sav - ior,

For our use Thy folds pre - pare; Bless - ed Je - sus,
Grace to cleanse and pow'r to free; Bless - ed Je - sus,
With Thy love our bo - soms fill; Bless - ed Je - sus,

From S. S. Hymnal, by per.

Bless - ed Je - sus, Thou hast bought us, Thine we are.
Bless - ed Je - sus, Let   us   ear - ly turn to Thee.
Bless - ed Je - sus, Thou hast lov'd us, love us still. A - MEN.

TUNE. "Savior, Like a Shepherd Lead us."

Anon.

1 In the vineyard of our Father
  Daily work we find to do;
  Scattered gleanings we may gather
  Though we are but young and few;
  Little clusters,
  Help to fill the garners too.

2 Toiling early in the morning
  Catching moments through the day,
  Nothing small or lowly scorning,
  While we work, and watch and pray;
  Gathering gladly,
  Freewill offerings by the way.

3 Not for selfish praise or glory,
  Not for objects nothing worth
  But to send the blessed story
  Of the gospel o'er the earth
  Telling mortals,
  Of our Lord and Savior's birth,

4 Steadfast then in our endeavor,
  Heavenly Father, may we be;
  And forever, and forever,
  We will give the praise to Thee,
  Hallelujah,
  Singing all eternity.

FREDERICK.

Anon.

FRED. L. MOREY.

1. Oh! Mighty King of Glo - ry, Thy chos-en her-ald send, To
2. Oh! Savior, bleeding, dy - ing, Thy deathless love re - veal, Un-
3. Oh! Savior, com-ing, reigning, Re - turn-ing to Thy throne, Thy

tell the old, old sto - ry, To earth's re - mot-est end, Give
til our-selves de - ny - ing, We burn with ho - ly zeal, Till
blood, Thy ban - ner stain - ing, A - wake, a-wake Thine own, Thy

hearts of love and pit - y, And will-ing, zeal - ous feet, Through
we our cross up - bear - ing, Shall bleed and die for Thee, Thy
vic - to - ry fore - see - ing, May we go forth and fight, Nor

for - est, plain and cit - y Thy mes - sage to re - peat.
ho - ly ser - vice shar - ing, From sin and self set free.
dream of ev - er flee - ing, Till Thou hast won the right.

AUTUMN.

JOHN FAWCETT. 1767.

1. Praise to Thee, Thou great Cre - a - tor! Praise to
2. For ten thou - sand bless - ings giv - en, For the

Thee from ev - 'ry tongue; { Join my soul with ev - 'ry
hope of fu - ture joy { Hail the God of our Sal -
{ Sound His praise thro' earth and
{ There en - rap - tur'd fall be -

FINE.

creature, Join the u - ni - ver - sal song. } Fa - ther,
va - tion! Praise Him for His love di - vine. }
heav-en, Sound Je - ho - vah's praise on high. } Joy - ful -
fore Him, Lost in won - der, love and praise, }

D.S.

source of all com - passion, Pure un - bound -ed grace is thine.
ly on earth a - dore Him, Till in heaven our song we raise.

Brightly.

1. Car - ol, sweetly car - ol, A Sav-ior born to - day;
2. Car - ol, sweetly car - ol, As when the an - gel throng
3. Car - ol, sweetly car - ol, The hap- py Christmas time;

Hear the joy-ful tid - ings, Oh, bear them far a - way;
O'er the vales of Ju - dah, A - woke the heav-'nly song;
Hark, the bells are peal - ing, Their mer - ry, mer - ry chime;

Car - ol, sweet-ly car - ol, Till earth's re - mot - est bound, Shall
Car - ol, sweet-ly car - ol, Good will with peace and love,
Car - ol, sweet-ly car - ol, Ye shin - ing ones a - bove,

From S. S. Hymnal, by per.

hear the mighty cho-rus, And e-cho back the sound.
Glo-ry in the high-est To God who reigns a-bove.
Sing in loud-est num-bers, Oh, sing re-deem-ing love.

CHORUS.

Car-ol, sweet-ly car - ol, car-ol sweet-ly to - day.
car - ol, car - ol, car-ol.

Car - ol sweet-ly, car - ol sweetly, to - day.

Bear the joy-ful tid-ings, Oh, bear them far a - way.

HOLLAND,

J. G. HOLLAND

GERMAN.

1. There's a song in the air! There's a
2. There's a tu - mult of joy, O'er the
3. In the light of that star, Lie the
4. We re - joice in the light, And we

star in the sky! There's a moth - er's deep
won - der - ful birth, For the Vir - gin's sweet
a - ges im - pearl'd, And that song from a -
ech - o the song, That comes down through the

prayer, And a ba - by's low cry!
boy, Is the Lord of the earth.
far, Has swept o - ver the world.
night, From the heav - en - ly throng.

By per. Chas. Scribner's Sons.

And the star rains its fire While the
Ay! the star rains its fire And the
Ev - ery hearth is a - flame And the
Ay! we shout, to the love - ly E -

Beau - ti - ful sing, For the man - ger of
Beau - ti - ful sing For the man - ger of
Beau - ti - ful sing, In the homes of the
van - gel they bring, And we greet in His

Beth - le - hem cra - dles a King.
Beth - le - hem cra - dles a King.
na - tions that Je - sus is King.
cra - dle our Sav - ior and King.

Anon.   ALBERTO RANDEGGER.

1. Come   to Je - sus, lit - tle one,   Come   to Je-sus now;
2. Seek   His face without de - lay;   Give Him now your heart;

Hum - bly at His gra-cious throne,   In submis - sion   bow.
Tar - ry not, but while you may,   Choose the bet - ter   part.

CHORUS.

At His feet con-fess your sin; Seek forgiveness there;

For His blood can make you clean, He will hear your prayer

HENRY ALFORD.

A. METHFESSEL, Arr. by B. C. F.

1. When in the Lord Je - ho - voh's name, The Sav-ior low - ly
2. We, too, are taught to know the Lord, To fear His name, to
3. Soon shall the Lord a - gain pass by To judgment, from His
4. Then may our youth-ful band be found, With cor - o - nels of

rid - ing came, Loud-est and first an in - fant throng, Greet-
read His word; And tho' we sim - ple are, and young, Can
throne on high; And from the Saints' as - sem - bled throng, Shall
tri - umph round, Rais-ing the heav'n - ly hosts a - mong, Our

ed His com-ing with their song: Ho - san - na in the High-est!
praise Him with our joy - ful song: Ho - san - na in the High-est!
burst up - on the world the song: Ho - san - na in the High-est!
cho - rus of e - ter - nal song: Ho - san - na in the High-est!

Mrs. F. H. DeWitt,   Carl Groos.

1. Hear the pen - nies drop - ping, List - en as they fall,
2. Now while we are lit - tle, Pen - nies are our store,

Ev - 'ry one for Je - sus, He will get them all.
But when we are old - er, We will give Him more;

Drop-ping, drop - ping ev - er, From each lit - tle hand,
Though we have not mon - ey, We can give Him love

'Tis our gift to Je - sus, From our miss - ion band.
He will own our off - 'ring, Smil-ing from a - bove.

136

SALVATION.

Rev. JOHN KING, 1830.

MOZART.

1. When, His Sal - va - tion bringing, To Zi - on Je - sus came,
2. And since the Lord re - tain-eth His love for chil -dren still,
3. For should we fail pro - claim-ing Our great Re-deem-er's praise

The chil - dren all stood sing - ing Ho - san - nas to His name,
Tho' now as King He reign-eth On Zi - on's heav'nly hill;
The stones our si - lence sham-ing, Would their Ho - san-nas raise.

Nor did their zeal of-fend him, But as he rode a - long,
We'll flock a-round His ban - ner, Who sits up - on His throne,
But shall we on - ly ren - der The trib - ute of our words?

He let them still at - tend Him And smiled to hear their song.
And cry a - loud, "Ho - san - na, To Da - vid's roy - al Son."
No, while our hearts are ten - der, They too shall be the Lord's.

TUNE, "Salvation."

Anon.

1 Lift high the royal standard,
   For Christ has saved from sin;
Upon the cross He suffered
   To bring Salvation in,
Go tell the heathen nations
   Who in their sorrows dwell,
That Christ, the Prince of Glory,
   Redeems from death and hell.

2 Filled with the love of Jesus,
   Our prayers like incense rise,
And Christ our royal Captain
   Is smiling from the skies.
The ark of God is moving,
   The heathen temples fall,
We'll take the world for Jesus,
   And crown Him Lord of all.

Bishop Heber, 1819.   Dr. Mason, 1823.

1. From   Green-lands i - cy   moun-tains, From In - dia's cor - al
2. What   though the spi - cy   breez - es Blow soft o'er Cey - lon's
3. Shall   we whose souls are   light - ed, With wis-dom from on
4. Waft,   waft ye winds His   sto - ry, And you, ye wa - ters,

strand, Where Af - ric's sun - ny foun-tains, Roll down their golden
isle,   Though ev - 'ry pros - pect pleas - es, And on - ly   man is
high,   Shall we   to men be - night ed, The lamp of life de -
roll,   Till like a sea of glo - ry, It spreads from pole to

sand; From man - y an an - cient riv - er From man - y a palm - y
vile; In vain with lav - ish kind - ness, The gifts of God   are
ny? Sal - va - tion, O sal - va - tion, The joy - ful sound pro -
pole; Till o'er our ran -somed na - ture, The Lamb for sin - ners

plain, They call us to de - liv - er, Their land from error's chain.
strewn, The hea-then in their blind - ness, Bow down to wood and stone.
claim, Till each re - mot-est na - tion Has heard Mes -si-ah's name.
slain, Re -deem-er, King, Cre - a - tor, In bliss re-turns to reign.

TUNE, "Missionary Hymn,"

THOMAS HASTINGS, 1830.

1 Now be the Gospel banner
   In every land unfurled,
   And be the shout "Hosanna!"
   Re-echoed through the world,
   Till every isle and nation,
   Till every tribe and tongue
   Receive the great salvation,
   And join the happy throng.

2 Yes—Thou shalt reign forever,
   O Jesus, King of kings,
   Thy light, Thy love, Thy favor,
   Each ransomed captive sings.
   The isles for Thee are waiting,
   The deserts learn Thy praise,
   The hills and valleys greeting,
   The song responsive raise:

TUNE, "Missionary Hymn."

IDA GLENWOOD.

1 God's vineyard is not bounded
   By ocean, sea, or shore;
   Go preach to every nation,
   The Christ whom you adore.
   Go teach the heathen mother
   The way of life and truth,
   And sow the seeds of wisdom
   In tender hearts of youth.

2 Our Master is our leader
   In every work of love;
   We may not pause or falter,
   He watches from above.
   And oh, what joy will thrill us
   In those bright fields of light;
   To meet the ransomed spirits
   From heathen lands of night.

By per. Woman's Baptist Miss. Soc. of the West.

WEBB.

Rev. Sam. F. Smith, 1831.

1. The morn-ing light is break-ing, The dark-ness dis-ap pears,
2. See hea-then na-tions bend-ing, Be-fore the God we love,
3. Blest riv-er of sal-va-tion, Pur-sue thine on-ward way,

The sons of earth are wak-ing To pen-i-ten-tial tears;
And thou-sand hearts as-cend-ing In grat-i-tude a-bove;
Flow thou to ev-'ry na-tion, Nor in thy rich-ness stay;

Each breeze that sweeps the o-cean Brings tidings from a-far,
While sin-ners now con-fess-ing, The Gospel call o-bey,
Stay not, till all the low-ly Triumphant reach their home;

Of na-tions in com-mo-tion, Pre-par'd for Zi-on's war.
And seek the Sav-ior's bless-ing, A na-tion in a day.
Stay not, till all the ho-ly Proclaim "The Lord is come."

JAMES EDMESTON.

1 Roll on, thou mighty ocean;
  And as thy billows flow,
Bear messengers of mercy
  To every land below.
Arise, ye gales, and waft them
  Safe to the destined shore;
That man may sit in darkness
  And death's black shade no more.

O Thou eternal Ruler,
  Who holdest in Thine arm
The tempests of the ocean,
  Protect them from all harm!
Thy presence, Lord, be with them,
  Wherever they may be:
Though far from us who love them,
  Still let them be with Thee.

TUNE, "Webb"

JAMES MONTGOMERY, 1822.

1 Hail to the Lord's anointed,
  Great David's greater Son!
Hail, in the time appointed,
  His reign on earth begun!
He comes to break oppression,
  To set the captive free;
To take away transgression,
  And rule in equity.

2 He comes with succor speedy,
  To those who suffer wrong;
To help the poor and needy,
  And bid the weak be strong;
To give them songs for sighing,
  Their darkness turn to light—
Whose souls condemned, and dying,
  Are precious in His sight.

3 For Him shall prayer unceasing,
  And daily vows ascend;
His kingdom still increasing,
  A kingdom without end.
The tide of time shall never
  His covenant remove;
His name shall live forever,
  That name to us is— Love.

STOCKWELL.

Rev. W. A. Muhlenberg, 1826.

Rev. Darius Eliot Jones. 1847.

1. Sav - ior, who Thy flock art feed - ing, With the
2. Now these lit - tle ones re - ceiv - ing, Fold them
3. Nev - er, from Thy pas - ture rov - ing, Let them
4. Then with - in Thy fold e - ter - nal, Let them

Shep - herd's kind - est care, All Thy peo - ple gent - ly
in Thy gra - cious arm; There, we know, Thy word be -
be the li - on's prey; Let Thy ten - der - ness, so
find a rest - ing place, Feed in pas - tures ev - er

lead - ing, While the lambs Thy bo - som share.
liev - ing, On - ly there se - cure from harm.
lov - ing, Keep them all life's dan - gerous way.
ver - nal, Drink the riv - ers, of Thy grace.

TUNE, "Stockwell.

THOMAS HASTINGS.

1 He that goeth forth with weeping,
    Bearing precious seed in love,
    Never tiring, never sleeping,
    Findeth mercy from above

2 Soft descend the dews of heaven,
    Bright the rays celestial shine;
    Precious fruits will thus be given,
    Through an influence all divine.

3 Sow thy seed, be never weary,
    Let no fears thy soul annoy;
    Be the prospect ne'er so dreary,
    Thou shalt reap the fruits of joy.

4 Lo, the scene of verdure brightening,
    See the rising grain appear!
    Look again! the fields are whitening,
    For the harvest time is near.

ZION.

W. WILLIAMS, 1772.

THOMAS HASTINGS, 1830.

1. O'er the gloom-y hills of darkness, Cheer'd by no ce-les-tial ray, Sun of right-eous-ness! a-ris-ing, Bring the bright, the glorious day; Send the gos-pel To the earth's re-mot-est day; Send the gos-pel To the earth's re-mot-est bound.

2. Kingdoms wide, that sit in darkness, Grant them, Lord, the glorious light; And from east-ern coast to west-ern, May the morn-ing chase the night; And re-demp-tion, Free-ly pur-chased, win the day; And re-demp-tion Free-ly pur-chased, win the day.

3. Fly a-broad, thou might-y gos-pel, Win and conquer, nev-er cease; May thy last-ing, wide do-min-ions, Mul-ti-ply and still in-crease. Sway Thy scep-tre, Sav-ior, all the world a-round; Sway Thy scep-tre, Sav-ior, all the world a-round.

TUNE. "St. Gertrude."
Page 8.

Abcu

1 Bear the message onward!
   Spread it far and wide;
   Let the distant nations
   Know that Jesus died;
   Died, that God might justly
   Sinners now forgive;
   Died, that through His merit,
   Guilty man might live.

CHORUS.

   Bear the message onward!
   Spread it far and wide;
   Let the distant nations
   Know that Jesus died.

2 Bear the message onward!
   Over land and sea;
   Nothing, save the Gospel,
   Makes men noble,—free.
   Spread, O spread the teaching
   Fraught with endless bliss;
   Angels well might covet
   Work so grand as this.—Cho.

3 Bear the message onward!
   'Tis so grandly true,
   Where-so-e'er it cometh
   Eden blooms anew.
   Work performed for Jesus
   Cannot go unblessed;
   Not till life is ended
   Must God's servants rest.—Cho.

TULLY.

Rev. Geo. Duffield, 1858.

Lowell Mason, 1860.

1. Stand up, stand up for Je - sus! Ye sol-diers of the cross;
2. Stand up, stand up for Je - sus! The trum-pet call o - bey,
3. Stand up, stand up for Je - sus! Stand in His strength a - lone,
4. Stand up, stand up for Je - sus! The strife will not be long;

Fine.

Lift high His roy - al ban - ner, It must not suf - fer loss;
D. S. Till ev - 'ry foe is van-quish'd, And Christ is Lord in - deed.
Forth to the might - y con - flict, In this His glo-rious day;
D. S. Your cour - age rise with dan - ger, And strength to strength op-pose.
The arm of flesh will fail you, Ye dare not trust your own;
D. S. When du - ty calls or dan - ger, Be nev - er want-ing there.
This day the noise of con - flict, The next the vic - tor's song;
D. S. He, with the King of glo - ry, Shall reign e - ter - nal - ly.

D. S.

From vic - t'ry un - to vic - t'ry, His ar - my shall He lead,
Ye that are men, now serve Him, A - gainst un-num-bered foes,
Put on the gos - pel ar - mor, And watch-ing un - to prayer,
To him that o - ver - com - eth, A crown of life shall be;

TUNE, "Jesus keep me near the Cross."

JOSEPHINE POLLARD, by per.

1 I was but a little lamb,
From the shepherd straying,
When I heard within my heart
Some one softly saying:—

CHORUS.
Follow me, follow me,
I will safely guide thee,
Through the stormy ways of life,
Walking close beside thee.

2 Never turning from that voice,
Never disobeying;
Let me know that unto me
Christ is ever saying;—CHO.

3 Early to His loving care
Shall my heart be given,
For each step I take with Him
Brings me nearer heaven.—CHO.

TUNE, "Tully."

Mrs. S. B. TITHERINGTON. In "Hymn Leaflet."

1 The voice of God is calling,
To all His ransomed host,
"March on! your foes are falling,
In vain their empty boast."
But haste! for souls are dying
For whom Christ Jesus bled,
And hungry souls are crying,
"O give us heavenly bread!"

2 The promised day is breaking,
The shadows flee apace;
When all the nations waking
Shall taste the Saviour's grace
Till bells in Christian steeples,
Shall ring from sea to sea;
And every country's peoples
To Jesus bow the knee.

By per. of Womans Baptist Miss. Soc. of the West.

148

CONTENTS.